THE WEST

WILL SWALLOW YOU

# THE WEST
# WILL SWALLOW YOU

*Essays*

LEATH TONINO

TRINITY UNIVERSITY PRESS
*San Antonio*

Published by Trinity University Press
San Antonio, Texas 78212

Copyright © 2019 by Leath Tonino

Cover design by ALSO
Book design by BookMatters, Berkeley
Author photo by Michael Price

Cover: *Sequoia National Park, Sept. 1957. Giant trees close to the Village. A cathedral in nature. Note figure close to central tree.* California. Matson Photo Service. www.loc.gov/item/mpc2009010336/PP.

ISBN 978-1-59534-903-3 paperback
ISBN 978-1-59534-904-0 ebook

Trinity University Press strives to produce its books using methods and materials in an environmentally sensitive manner. We favor working with manufacturers that practice sustainable management of all natural resources, produce paper using recycled stock, and manage forests with the best possible practices for people, biodiversity, and sustainability. The press is a member of the Green Press Initiative, a nonprofit program dedicated to supporting publishers in their efforts to reduce their impacts on endangered forests, climate change, and forest-dependent communities.

The paper used in this publication meets the minimum requirements of the American National Standard for Information Sciences—Permanence of Paper for Printed Library Materials, ANSI 39.48-1992.

CIP data on file at the Library of Congress

23  22  21  20  19    |    5  4  3  2  1

*For my sister—*
*fellow explorer of childhood's back fields*

This aimless shifting east and west,
I even have to laugh myself.
But how else can I make
The whole world my home?
—Baisao

# Contents

# Preface

Start with that little word, that big country: *West.*

I grew up far from there, along the shores of Lake Champlain, between Vermont's Green Mountains and New York's Adirondacks. Having supported myself as a freelance scribbler for the past ten years, I can now survey my publication record and note just how important this region of mosses and otters and gray clouds has been to my writing, not to mention my sleeping, eating, laughing, crying, questioning, questing, and ongoing education in the art of aimless appreciative wandering.

That said, it would be difficult to deny that I am, borrowing Gary Snyder's term, "promiscuous" with ecosystems. Despite my love of the Northeast's intricate communities, despite my enduring passion for looking and looking again at the valley that raised me, despite my admiration for rooted authors who sing the praises of their native ground—well, these feet of mine do get mighty itchy, and the best scratch apparently comes from traveling many miles over ever-changing terrain.

I've rambled the American West this past decade, keeping the land's vibrant pulsing front and center in my experience. I felt it on Arizona's remote Kaibab Plateau, where I worked as a biologist studying elusive raptors, and on San Francisco's pigeon-flocked park benches, where I trained myself to resist the false, dangerous, strangely seductive notion that the civilized and the wild are fundamentally opposed. I felt it on Wyoming ranches, at Nevada campsites, all through Colorado's burly ranges. I felt it in libraries and national monuments, in people, in a midnight fox's eyes, in the rushing wind. Broadly speaking, *The West Will Swallow You* is about that pulse of a planet often buried under blacktop and cast in bluish screen-glow, but nonetheless present, relentlessly present.

Of course, complications arise when gathering together a bunch of pieces that were initially created to stand alone in magazines and journals. Harmonizing them is a tall order, an impossible order. I keep reminding myself that this isn't a single, coherent narrative, but a gaggle, a sprawl, and that the diversity of tones and topics should be seen as an attribute, not a flaw. Perhaps it's fitting to pair reported stories with personal reflections, conventional texts with experimental lists, restrained sorrow with freewheeling humor. Introducing *Eagle Pond*, a bundle of his previously scattered essays, Donald Hall puts it nicely: "But these different voices are each my own voice—and Picasso said that every human being is a colony."

My advice is to read, or at least *attempt* to read, the following pages with the same spirit of random curious searching that characterized their composition. While the collection allows for a conventional front-to-back journey, there's no reason that it can't also function as a vagabond's companion, a browser's buddy, like that atlas you pick up, leaf through, set down, repeat. Why not get a little lost, as I have? Why not scratch your feet?

To close this opening, let me drop a final quote. In an interview, Robert Bringhurst discusses how landscapes—specific forests, coastlines, and the like—can function as major characters in the yarns that humans spin, the tales we tell. But then he pauses, and from that pause emerges an intriguing thought: "I wonder, though, what percentage of the world's novels take place entirely indoors. I'll bet it's much larger than the portion set almost entirely outdoors."

Reviewing these travels, these years, these white sheets of paper stained by my unruly ink, by my effort and play, I notice lots of sky and weather, lots of dirt and stone, lots of feather and fur, lots of flowing water and falling snow, lots of green growth and shadowy stillness. Setting the book "almost entirely outdoors" wasn't intentional. Nope. The boots have their own ideas regarding where to go and when, and the pen has its own itinerary. This is the life they lead because...

*Lub-dub. Lub-dub. Lub-dub.*
The heart, the earth.
There it is again—that pulse.

# CALIFORNIA

## The West Will Swallow You

I took a train from Richmond, along the rim of San Pablo Bay, across the Central Valley. Egrets stood in flooded rice fields bordering the track, still and white like flags on a windless day. Friends picked me up in Rocklin and we continued by car to Lake Tahoe, then farther south. Sharp peaks. Winding roads. I dug a cave in a snowbank that evening and slept inside the hollow. It felt good to be out of the city and good to squirm into the cave's mute darkness. I slept, quite literally, like a bear, removed from all things, even the stars.

The next morning was Sunday, sunny and golden. We went skiing. We talked and joked for hours up above the trees, on the chairlift and in the alpine bowls. I hadn't seen my friends in a couple of months and hadn't skied in a couple of years. I lacked skill, but that hardly mattered. By midafternoon we were exhausted, glad to be loading the car, glad for the drive out of the mountains, down to the sunset. I changed into jeans and sneakers, careful not to dirty my socks in the parking lot's mud. We passed a single beer around, trading sips.

Upslope, a young man was just beginning to die.

We didn't know it at the time. We only knew that there

was a competition on the mountain, a huge, steep wall of stone and clinging snow opened this one day to the world's elite freeskiers. Resting between runs, we had watched tiny specks charge the shadowed face. Cornice, couloir, cliff— the specks rode these features with apparent ease, skiing air and earth in equal measure. Crowds cheered. Crowds stared. I remember saying to my friends that these were the most impressive athletes I'd ever seen. What would it feel like to ski that way, to give oneself over so completely to gravity's great pull?

We passed the beer, finished it off. I said something about uncertainty, something about the way those skiers up there on the shadowed face made an art and a life out of balancing control and its opposite.

Yeah, my friends said. No doubt.

Like that, we got in the car, buckled up, drove away.

～

My friends are old friends, childhood friends from Vermont. I've romped with Will since I was four and Tucker since I was five. Twenty-odd years later we're still Vermonters, but we're out west—working, exploring, trying in earnest to find our way through the muddle of adulthood. We call our families on Sundays and ask about the weather, what the leaves are doing, how the ice is forming on the lake. In our prolonged absence, the dogs that were our brothers and sisters grow tired and are put down. Condominiums sprout in pastures where cows once grazed. Rocks slide. Trees fall. We talk for that hour on Sunday, visit in December, maybe in the summer. Then it's back to the Sierra Nevada or the Grand Canyon or wherever.

When I left Vermont at eighteen people told me I'd never

return. Sometimes it felt like a warning, sometimes more like a prophecy. *The West will swallow you, as a canyon swallows stones.* I assured everybody that I was just going to college, just Colorado, and I'd return shortly. *The West will swallow you, and you will swallow the West, its space and sky, its ranges and their storms.* Obviously, these are my words. I don't remember exactly how they put it. Rather, I remember the mood, the intensity, and that it all seemed silly. I was young and my life held no such drama. Vermont was home. Colorado was a journey. *The West is big. Its beauty and loneliness are powers you do not understand. The West has absorbed so many young men like you.*

A young man like me is indeed interested in beauty and loneliness and powers he does not understand. A young man like me sleeps in a sleeping bag as often as he does a regular bed. A young man like me climbs mountains in poor weather to learn what that entails. He sleeps on summits. He rises at dawn. He sets hammocks high in trees and sleeps in swaying crowns. He sleeps in canyons, by rivers, on schist. He sleeps in snowcaves, in imitation of bears.

I won't say they were wrong, my dentist and my friend's dad and whoever else, but neither will I say they were correct. What I'll say is that I've been wandering for nearly a decade, all through the alphabet, from AZ to CA to UT to WY, the whole time living cheap, saving up. I plan to buy some land in the East, preferably without a road to it, preferably with a stream. Beside that stream I daily build a cabin in my mind. No matter where I go, the cabin follows. It's a small room through which the seasons flow, and with them the local animals, the winged seeds, the flowers and gusts of rain. Low clouds. Loons. I love Vermont. I love the cornfields and migrating snow geese. I love the orange newts walking slow beneath endless ferns. I intend to die there, right where I was born, though I know this is not mine to decide.

My mother lived in Tucson for two years postcollege and left when she realized she might stay. A job. A man. A desert in bloom. She figured these would become a life for her and she worried about that. Her place was New England. She needed to get back.

A neighbor from my childhood—a friend since toddler days—graduated from the same college I did in Colorado. He lives in Denver. He mentioned to me a while ago that he could never again live east of the Mississippi. He's a skier. He's been swallowed. He skis every weekend for a solid half of the year.

~

Will emailed me the article from the newspaper two days after Ryan died. Ryan was the one the paramedics crouched around and leaned over and struggled to save while I changed my pants in a muddy parking lot at the mountain's base. He was twenty-five. He grew up two towns north of us in Vermont. His love was freeskiing and he was talented, a natural athlete, a hard worker, an alert, generous, focused young man who smiled often. In reading of his life I was inspired. Here was a peer—a version of myself—who loved and pursued his love. He pursued it all through the West, up to that moment when it swallowed his life.

We had some of the same coaches growing up, some of the same friends.

The inspiration faded and I stared through the computer.

My sister emailed me, asking if I'd heard. My sister is a

skier. She lives in Vermont and teaches at the high school we both attended. She left the state when she was eighteen. Stinking cows, she would say. She went to Baltimore, dated a guy from the projects who had been shot during a drive-by and who had miraculously recovered. Now she owns a house and a dog and skis two or three days a week all winter long. She skis some of the hills we skied as little kids. Her house is not a cabin, but it is small, and its windows do frame the flow of seasons and much more.

*Can you imagine that sunny day being your last on earth?* She asked and she was right—it had been sunny, golden. I couldn't respond. I tried. I couldn't. A line from a poem by Alberto Rios came to me: "Words are our weakest hold on the world." Of course, I couldn't write that either. Some minutes passed. I stared through the screen's glowing blank page and a second poem came to me, a haiku from Matsuo Bashō: "Deep as the snow is, / Let me go as far as I can / Till I stumble and fall, / Viewing the white landscape."

Bashō was swallowed by his Zen practice, by poetry, by the world beneath and above and surrounding the two. He left his hut and belongings and friends, returned to them, left them again. He heard the call, answered the call, rambled thousands of miles across Japan with just a paper raincoat to shield him from the storms of cherry blossoms, the uncertainty of it all. He traveled the narrow road, northward, to the interior, through the mountains.

∼

Words are our weakest hold on the world, and I've got nothing new to say about the West. Long hours on long roads, shirt off, windows down, wind sounds, pipe tobacco bitter on the tongue—these drives remind me of what I've always known, what I think we all have always known, that joy and sadness are one, as the mesa and sky are one, welded together by a molten setting sun.

I toss a plate of red sandstone into the Grand Canyon, listening for a landing that never comes. How many Vermonts would this emptiness absorb before cornfields and snow geese and endless ferns overflowed the sagebrush rim? I picture Camel's Hump, a peak in the Green Mountains that is dear to me and has been forever. I've slept on its summit countless times, alone and with friends, in winter and summer, in a tent and in a snowcave. I picture a giant hand, some cartoonishly gigantic deity's hand swooping from the unbroken blue sky, plucking up my special mountain, dropping it into the canyon. I picture my cabin, the one I've not yet built, disappearing.

I toss another rock and wonder. How many lives have been swallowed by this canyon? How many young men have fallen here, either in love with beauty and loneliness and powers they do not understand, or when a loose bit of ledge crumbled out from underfoot? The Grand Canyon is a killer. The statistics say that young men are the most likely to get into trouble. There are signs at trailheads warning that people like me are most likely to die. It's the same year after year, sign after sign, rock after rock.

I throw another. I throw another. I sense my body falling with them.

There is a fear in me, beside the fear of dying. It is the fear of being swallowed against my will—swallowed by a place.

~

We took a snaky road out of the mountains that Sunday in order to avoid the ski traffic headed for Sacramento and the

Bay Area. Snowbanks fifteen feet tall rose sheer from the blacktop, smooth as marble walls. The road was a hallway, a sinuous slot reminiscent of those I'd scrambled in Utah and Arizona. The blacktop had melted clean with the day's bright hours.

I sat in the middle seat in the back, my view through the windshield framed by shoulders—Will on the left, Tucker on the right. Ponderosa pines, their branches pillowed, reached out over the road, into the frame. We were not listening to music. No one was talking. The sun was in our eyes and a happy fatigue moved among us, thick and soft like honey.

Icy peaks. Twists and turns. I was almost dozing, easing toward it, when something beyond the windshield—some motion—called me from that honeyed edge. It was one of the pines. A bird had touched it, or maybe wind, or maybe neither of these. Snow fell from a single branch. Light came through the snow, silvering each grain. The branch sprang up. I sprang up. Then it was done and we were down the road.

～

I have nothing new to say about the West. It swallows some of us. It swallows us in different ways. Reading the article, remembering a peer I never met, an inspired young man who loved and pursued his love, who gave himself to gravity's great pull, who moved with power and ease on a mountain's shadowed face, I felt something—something immense—and the feeling left me staring through the screen.

I tried to write my sister, but stumbled and fell, viewing the white landscape.

I closed my eyes.

It was the welded joy-sadness, that's all. It was never making it home. It was the dangerous, enlivening, many-mouthed land, the notion that we are winged seeds drifting over hungry scratches of earth. It was inarticulate, an image, the branch releasing its snow, the light coming through, the grains silvering for an instant before falling to the warm black road, melting away, keeping no space.

Dropping. Darkening. Central Valley again. I didn't know what time it was or what towns we'd passed through. I didn't even know I'd been asleep. No music played. Nobody spoke. There were egrets out there, white birds like flags of peace. I couldn't see them. Or perhaps I could, just barely, only if I didn't really look, didn't really try.

# Letter to the Megalopolis

Tonight I will be your eyes and through me you will watch the moonrise and together we will be slowed and stilled and humbled. I will walk your puddled streets through traffic-roar and siren-wail, will climb the hill that is your shoulder, will climb and climb until the buildings release their boxy grip and the sidewalk becomes a trail. Up there, in a small park, balanced on a rock above your sprawling, glowing body, I will pull back my hood and look to the east.

We won't blink.

We'll hardly breathe.

Have you seen the color orange? Tonight you will. You will see it bleeding from the orange of yourself, your grid of lamps and windows and neon signs. You will see a giant circle of orange inching up from behind the far ridge, a circle of orange larger and greater than me or you, than the ridge or anything. At first it will be scary, this heavy, rising presence. We won't like it, the way it makes us flutter, our attention beating against craters and dry seabeds, our eyes like moths. We won't like it, but neither will we shy away.

I'm telling you, Megalopolis, this is going to be some night. The orange moon will arc into the sky, carrying us with it, me right up out of my shoes, you right up out of your concrete, broken glass, poverty, cigarette smoke, excess, idiotic wealth. By degrees the orange moon will shrink and fade, fade and shrink, and then at last the lamps and windows and neon signs will glow bright again.

We will return to earth.

We will return to this earth, changed.

I've been with you for a long time now, five winters and five springs, and it's always good, always bad, always all kinds of things, all kinds of everything. But you know. You're you. The helicopters chop. The rapist goes about his business. The newspapers arrive each dawn. The money is made and counted and counted again. The clock ticks over our heads and on our wrists and in our temples, as if the ticking were our pulse. You know these facts. You are the ticking.

And you also know that there are children with innocent faces, children playing games, children laughing. And that there are hawks nesting in pines bordering the playgrounds. And that there are gophers eating tiny flowers, nibbling silky petals. You know it's all kinds of things, all kinds of everything, and that the moon does visit regularly, though of course the moon never stays.

Megalopolis, enough. We both understand that I can't be your eyes, and you have no ears, so I can't even read you this letter. Really, it's not you who needs humbling anyway. This letter is for me. This letter is for me and the people I haven't met, the people I will never meet, the people I wish the best for nonetheless. We've forgotten the moon. We are screen-dazed and sad. We are lost in a room, the walls closing ever inward, the computer's blue light ghosting across our features. There is a faint electric hum. There is a wailing siren at the door.

But the door opens onto nothing.

And the door is locked.

Here I am at the heart of you, surrounded by you, alone. Here I am ascending the shoulder, balancing atop the rock, pulling back my hood. The moon is rising fat, fiery, an orange beast to crush the distant hills. Impossible, it would seem, to ever in a million years forget such a moon, such a presence. Impossible, but somehow we do.

Okay. Time to finish this letter. Time to say fondly, sincerely, best, take care. Time to be quiet, to forget time, to taste orange and watch and keep watching and swallow hard.

And swallow hard.

And swallow harder than before.

# A Room of Boughs
# in a City of Lights

I loaded my backpack with supplies for a three-night trip: hammock, sleeping bag, hundred-foot rope, rock-climbing harness, carabiners and webbing, raingear, headlamp, six peanut butter sandwiches, a twenty-dollar bill, a knife in case I got tangled in my rigging and had to cut myself free. It was already afternoon when I left my apartment on Dolores Street and pushed west, uphill, toward Twin Peaks. Mockingbirds talked across the sky. Babies babbled from their strollers. And the trees, as anticipated, were bountiful, beautiful, and diverse. Mike Sullivan, an obsessed amateur botanist and author of the field guide *The Trees of San Francisco*, has identified 274 species growing in the city. There are Washington thorns and cockspur coral trees; jacarandas, cajeputs, and Chinese photinias; sweetshades and golden rain trees; spotted and lemon-scented gums; pin, cork, and holly oaks. Mostly, I didn't know the names of what I saw— but it wasn't names that I intended to climb.

My plan was really more of a prompt, a nudge in the direction of urban-arboreal adventure. I'd wander San Francisco, neighborhood to neighborhood, park to park, paying attention to trees. I'd pay attention to ants and squirrels and clouds and my own shifting thoughts as well—but primarily I'd focus on the trees. When I found one I liked, probably a big one, I'd climb it, string the hammock as high as possible, and lose myself in the dazed sway and drifty weave of green smells, green sounds, green moods. This would be a new city, a lofted metropolis of branch and twig. I'd rock to bed, wake with dawn's birds, rappel to earth, and go get a cup of coffee. Maybe I'd be downtown, at Union Square or Embarcadero. Maybe I'd be in the Presidio or bordering the zoo.

Strolling, I noticed the particularities of the trees I passed. Magnolias I'd walked by a hundred times demanded consideration. A ginkgo with yellowing leaves stopped me in my tracks. By creating a situation in which I needed a tree to camp in, a situation in which the *lack* of a tree rendered me just your average tramp, I'd tricked my mind into a new type of attunement. Crown structure, location relative to buildings and power lines, degree of rot in dead and dying limbs—all of this was now important. I stared, scrutinized, kept moving. The perfect one was out there, somewhere.

I made a mental map of trees I could come back to should nothing better turn up. A California pepper tree in the Castro had a sweet umbrella shape to it but leaned against a second-story window that I worried was someone's bathroom. A ring of eucalyptus on Tank Hill promised amazing views of the Financial District, but the trees themselves were unappealing, their hammock sites few and daunting. I liked one Monterey cypress, but when I traced the trunk downward it disappeared behind a fence, into a backyard. This got me thinking. The cypress's roots extended beneath the street—I imagined them pulsing with water and nutrients

below the blacktop—and visually the bulk of the tree inhabited an airy public space. So whose tree was it? I got a
bit miffed: *To hog a tree like that! To lock it away and deny
it a hammocker's companionship!* At the same time, I was
conscious of the dubious legality of my whole enterprise.
Best to leave it alone, I figured, find privacy amid denser
vegetation.

Norfolk Island pine (too flexy). Cliff date palm (too
frondy). Tree by tree I worked my way to the top of the
Mount Sutro Open Space Reserve, a largely undeveloped
area of sixty acres at the city's center. The afternoon was
ebbing, my anxiety about establishing a place to sleep rising. I followed a shuttle bus into an apartment complex
where the trees, mostly eucalyptus, were out of my league,
ascension-wise. I'd learned technical tree-climbing techniques while working for the US Forest Service on a study
of northern goshawks, but that's not to say I'm confident
around either heights or knots; climbing is intense work
and generally not to be messed with after dark.

I needed to discover my perfect tree. And soon.

⁓

The coast redwood is a Northern California icon; it's the
sparkle in John Muir's eye, the poet Jane Hirshfield's "great
calm being." As a human's body provides an immense terrain for mites and other roaming microcritters, a redwood's
body provides habitat for warblers and salamanders and
epiphytes. Redwoods can grow to over three hundred feet
and live more than a thousand years. They're skyscrapers,
*fogscrapers*, animate towers with corridors and chambers
and balconies and elevator shafts and fire escapes. It probably comes as no surprise that seeking a hammock-hotel

there atop Mount Sutro, I found myself checking in at the trunk of *Sequoia sempervirens.*

Mine was one hundred feet tall, by no means a monster, but then again, an absolute monster. It made a lamp-post look like a puny sapling and rose considerably higher than the four-story apartment buildings across the street. A friendly monster, it spoke to me, called me up into the complicated heights. The language was presence, massive and inviting, not heard but felt. I know it's unscientific and weird, but this is the truth: *Hey there, little fella,* the tree said, *why don't you grab that branch of mine and see where it leads?*

The redwood isn't only a major Bay Area player; it's also the quintessential adventure tree, a botanical Everest. In college, about the time I started hanging hammocks higher than three feet off the ground (I was into rock climbing and forest ecology), I read an article in the *New Yorker* that documented the search for the world's tallest trees. Written by Richard Preston, the article profiled Humboldt State University biologist Stephen Sillett, a guy who spends days and nights in the canopy living out of a harness and a hammock. Preston's book on the subject, *The Wild Trees,* argues that the upper tiers of a redwood forest are as little understood as the depths of the ocean. Hyperion, the tallest tree on earth at 379 feet, stands in an undisclosed locale in the backcountry of Redwood National and State Parks. Epic storms, Tyrolean traverses, automobile-sized chunks of debris crumbling above helmeted scientists—I burned through *The Wild Trees* in a weekend.

Organizing my gear and nerves in the duff beside the sidewalk, I kept reminding myself that I'm no Steve Sillett, no expert, and that I needed to be methodical and slow.

Overhead, innumerable branches radiated out from the redwood's straight bole in a maze of ladders, the lowest ones almost within reach. With all those holds I wouldn't need the rope, just the harness system and my own monkey style. By anchoring loops of webbing to limbs as I climbed, I could inch upward without ever risking a major fall. I might slip, knock my noggin, and dangle stunned for a spell, but plummeting to my death was out of the question. Once I left the ground, the harness would never loosen, not for sleeping, not for peeing, not for anything. In a sense, the tree would protect me from its own dangers.

I double-knotted my shoelaces, tucked my shirt in, jumped for a branch, missed it, jumped again, pulled, contorted, and got it underfoot. A young lady in a purple jacket walked by and I held my breath; though I was plainly visible, ten feet away and no more than eight feet high, she didn't see me. A man with a briefcase passed, then a grandma with a toddler and shopping bags, then another shuttle bus. Nobody glanced up. So quickly, I'd crossed over to the secret city.

⁓

You scrape legs and hands, get needles in your hair, hook branches with elbows, armpits, ankles, and knees. You impress yourself on the tree and the tree impresses itself on you. It's like Robert Frost's apple-picking poem, the one where an "instep arch not only keeps the ache, / It keeps the pressure of a ladder-round." Your body learns the tree though this touching, this ache and pressure. There's mysterious reciprocity here, deep rapport between beings.

Recall that image of a mite orienteering the landscape of a human body. Climbing higher, I went small and the tree went large. The other world—Below or The Ground or The City I Previously Knew—dropped off like so many fluttering bark chips. Sure, sounds filtered through the walls of foliage (sirens, kids yelling), but they were vague, less than real, coming to me the way an alarm clock's beeping enters a dream. The *real* was at hand, was the wood in my hand: this hold and the next hold and the next.

After approximately eighty feet (the tree's collarbone?) I stopped, my attention drawn from the climbing for the first time in a half-hour or longer. Something pink caught my eye through a window in the boughs—the bay reflecting the sunset sky, a huge view of toy-sized cargo ships and the Oakland Hills. I looked around and another window opened to the north—the Golden Gate Bridge, Mount Tamalpais spilling ridges to the Pacific, folds of land fading into the distance. I'd been in the meditative do-not-fall trance, the trance of effort and exhaustion, and was at last awakening. A red-breasted nuthatch landed nearby, gleaned an insect, and dissolved back to green. Again the tree spoke: *This is your spot, little fella. Make yourself at home.*

It took another half-hour of tiptoeing to rig the hammock, stressing the whole time about bobbling a key piece of gear and watching it plummet. When the chores were finished, my supplies hung on lines I'd strung up, like a kitchen in Tuscany with herbs and salamis and saucepans dangling from the ceiling. I removed sneakers and socks to let my sweaty feet dry against the tree's cool, rough skin. Swinging in my harness, testing various seats, scheming a way to recline across three branches, a part of me wondered if the hammock was necessary.

Two scrub jays stopped by for a chat. I ate a peanut butter

sandwich and watched the city's lights lift from the gloaming in reds, oranges, and electric blues. It got darker. A neon glow leaked through the gaps and cracks in the foliage walls. I ate a second sandwich and flipped on my headlamp. The top was a mere twenty feet away.

~

The trip went on for another three days, with overnights in a wind-tortured, rain-lashed cypress by the ocean, and a redwood in Golden Gate Park that let me gain fifty feet before scaring me down to a cramped hammock site. I mingled with the homeless, walked dozens of miles, bought a slice of pizza, studied trees from afar, from below, from inside and out. Each was different, a unique vehicle providing access to itself and to some new perspective on the city. A series of engagements! A sequence of invitations! Oh, but nothing beat that initial Mount Sutro redwood, the adventure's literal and figurative high point. I can close my eyes and go there, even now.

The trunk tapered to the diameter of my wrist and I perched on a branch the diameter of my thumb, then touched the utmost tiptop for good measure. I tied in twice to be safe, and in fact I *was* safe—no threat of creeps or thieves, no fear of getting hit by a van in the crosswalk. The night embraced me like a fat firm hug.

A dog barked. A parked car idled. I watched an elderly couple preparing dinner in one of the apartments across the street, watched the city lights, watched my brain's activity slide into rest. Hirshfield's line about a "great calm being" came back to me, and for a while that's how I felt—like a redwood, both great and calm. It was mellowness by association, I guess.

Soft. Still.

Nobody on earth—no human, at least—knew my whereabouts.

Again, it's weird and unscientific, but paused there in that soupy darkness a hundred feet off the ground, the thought came to me: *I never asked this tree for permission*. In my excitement—over the ascent, then over the camp chores—I'd forgotten my manners.

So I started to say something, some thanks and praise, some gratitude for offering me this experience. Hearing the words aloud though, I shut up. Or maybe the tree shut me up? I felt silly, not because I was talking to a plant, but because I was only now realizing that I'd been talking to a plant all along; I'd heard the redwood's voice, why wouldn't it have heard mine? Anything that needed saying had already been said, and, moreover, said with a clarity human words rarely achieve. It was the clarity of climbing, of touching. It was the language of bodies, of presence. My host knew everything I was thinking. I *knew* it knew this— don't ask me how.

The dog barked. The elderly couple stirred their soup. The city glittered.

I descended to my cozy hanging bed, my lullaby of a hammock.

# Secret Springs

I met Joel Pomerantz at a bustling intersection in Cole Valley, the geographic heart of San Francisco. All around us the usual morning crowds were up to their usual morning business: fiddling with smartphones, waiting in line for brunch, hopping on and off buses, fiddling with smartphones. If anybody besides Pomerantz was thinking about water—where it comes from, where to find it, how it can draw us into an intimate relationship with the local cityscape—it wasn't apparent.

"We've got options," Pomerantz said. "Head into Sutro Forest and look at a true gushing spring, a really nice spot, or, if you want something more urban, climb over the ridge at the end of this street to a site where water wells up from beneath the pavement." I voted for the latter, picturing a microparadise of ferns and flowers bursting through cracks in the sidewalk. "Good call," he said. "The ones in plain sight are often the most interesting."

Pomerantz—a thirty-four-year resident of the city and the founder of Thinkwalks ("Nerdy Tours for San Franciscans")—is, in his own words, "a hands-on freelance educator of the public with a special interest in fresh water and water politics." He is also that wonderful and necessary subspecies: a nonconformist, a guy in a bright yellow T-shirt and red knit cap pausing now and then to put his ear to a sewer access cover and listen for gurgles. "I've always resisted having a career," he told me, explaining that underemployment affords a person lots of opportunities to wander. "You can't depend on experts. You have to become a part of the environment yourself."

Outside a hardware store, we stopped to consider what to my eye resembled nothing but traffic and more phone-fiddling pedestrians. "This used to be all dunes," Pomerantz said with a sweep of the hand. He reminisced about first coming across a black-and-white photo, taken in the nineteenth century, that shows a pool of water backed up against sand and grass. "It was a dynamic feature called Laguna Seca. That means Dry Lake. It came and went, depending on conditions." I mentioned that his reality seemed doubled, the past no less vivid than the present, and he agreed: "I hallucinate dunes when I ride my bike through town. I see the gullies, the drainages, and I notice the infrastructure on top and how it all connects."

Though we never consulted it, Pomerantz carried a rolled-up topographic map, sometimes swinging it like a baton, sometimes tucking it into his armpit. It was his most recent project: Seep City, a survey of paved-over creeks, backfilled wetlands, tidal sloughs, municipal reservoirs, half-hidden brooks, and dozens of secret springs. In addition to data gleaned from photos in library archives, the map is derived from government surveys conducted in the Gold Rush era. More than anything though, it's a product of boots-on-the-ground "landscape sleuthing." Pomerantz has found a number of damp basements and soggy backyards

by knocking on doors and introducing himself to strangers.
He estimates that he's initiated five thousand—or perhaps
ten thousand—random conversations on the street over
the years, searching for clues.

Forty-five minutes into our stroll, having worked our
way through crooked neighborhoods and discussed everything from bike activism to desert wilderness travel to an
outfit called the Awesome Foundation (somehow it came
as no surprise that Pomerantz was on the board of the San
Francisco chapter), we reached our destination: an empty
parking lot fronting a three-story apartment building. By
the appearance of it, five or six reasonably hydrated guys
had recently gone pee nearby, their trickles gathering into
a snake that slithered twenty-five feet and culminated in a
millimeter-deep puddle. "It's always flowing," Pomerantz
said, crouching to touch the wet blacktop with his fingertip.

What we'd found was a freshwater spring: both entirely
unimpressive and, because of what it represented—namely,
a kind of primeval lifeblood that will not die no matter how
much civilization we heap atop it—totally inspiring. For a
moment, I sensed thousands of liquid threads coursing beneath my feet, vibrating in drainpipes and dark tunnels of
rock.

"The world we live in is a real place, and it's worth real
effort, real exploration," Pomerantz said, his finger still
against the pavement. "You've got to go far beyond the edge
of the computer screen, far beyond the armchair."

# Watching Goggles

It's a typical late-summer afternoon in San Francisco, chilly and damp, the sky a low ceiling of cloud. I'm sitting at the edge of a golf course fairway with Janet Kessler—waiting, watching, listening. The soft *thowck* of a well-struck ball sounds from behind a screen of Monterey cypress at our back. A red-tailed hawk alights on a nearby branch. "It's funny," Kessler says, scanning the expanse of cropped grass before us. "People are always asking me how to see a coyote in the city. I tell them the coyotes are right here, right in front of you. You just have to look."

And so we look.

*Thowck.*

A naturalist, self-taught urban wildlife photographer, and longtime resident of San Francisco, Kessler, age sixty-five, has spent much of the past decade tracking, studying, documenting, and generally enjoying the heck out of her favorite neighbor, *Canis latrans.* She spends a minimum of three hours a day, usually at dawn or dusk, checking up on individual animals and family packs. By her estimate, several dozen coyotes live in the metropolis: "McLaren, Lake Merced, Golden Gate—they're in all the parks." This golf course, sandwiched between a neighborhood flush with

Chinese restaurants and a cliff band that drops steeply to the Pacific, is one of her go-to sites.

She points to a tee box on a slight rise to our left, indicating that I should hold my gaze there. "Goggles usually comes out around six or seven p.m., though I've seen him as early as four p.m. He's the coyote I've known the longest, almost eight years. He looks a little like he's hanging on his bones now—he walks stiff—but hey, we all get old."

*Thowck.*

Two border collies approach with a young guy in tow. "Have you seen the coyote?" Kessler asks.

"All the time," the guy says. "It yells at us." He plays a video on his phone of a coyote standing beside a log, framed by shrubs, barking. The border collies turn, intrigued.

"Oh, yeah, that's Goggles all right," Kessler says. "I recognize my coyotes by facial structure and expressions, not by their fur. It's the same with humans. We hardly ever forget a face."

Some people take on their dog's appearance and mannerisms after enough years together—a beefy, truculent man jogging his pit bull, a poodle in the lap of a prim, curly-haired lady. Kessler is thin, quick, and hyperattentive, her descriptions of coyotes often more pantomime than speech. She dresses in various shades of muted green to blend with her surroundings: mossy jeans, fern-colored fleece, olive ball cap with a coyote standing above the brim. A brown-gray ponytail hangs to her lumbar spine, resembling—as the name suggests—a tail.

There is a surefire way to identify Kessler as human, though, and that's the massive camera in its case, slung across her chest like a camo-patterned infant. "I don't have an encounter every time I come out, but if I do, I'll easily get six hundred photos," she says. "My camera is my notebook. It records time, place, weather, behavior." Her images have been featured in Bay Area magazines and shown at local museums and galleries, but they are first and foremost personal research tools. Recently, she's been using them in conjunction with Google Maps to better comprehend how coyotes navigate the city—what she calls "trekking patterns."

Kessler's obsession can be traced back to a random accident. In 2006 she cut her finger on a can of black beans and had to quit practicing the pedal harp for two hours each day, her habit at the time. During the recovery, while walking her dog on Twin Peaks, a semi-wild ridge at the center of the city, she happened upon a hunting coyote. Entranced by its behavior, she returned the next morning with her camera—and the next morning, and the next. Shortly, she had self-published an album, *Myca of Twin Peaks,* and was feeling an entwined sense of wonder and responsibility, an obligation to share her newfound appreciation of San Francisco's lesser-known denizens.

Occasionally, coyotes in urban and suburban settings have attacked dogs and even people, but Kessler argues that such antagonistic interactions are avoidable. She's adamantly opposed to trapping and killing programs, and helped found a volunteer group—Coyote Coexistence—to educate the public about how to live alongside the species. (Rule number one: Keep your dog leashed.) "In every community, there's one group that wants to kill them, one that wants to save them," she says. *Coyotes as Neighbors*—the title of the thirty-minute slideshow she produced for coyotecoexistence.com—is an apt summary of her hopeful vision.

*Thowck.*

And now here comes one of those neighbors: Goggles.

Kessler is on her feet in an instant, camera out, shutter snapping. Goggles, so named because the coat rimming his eyes is "a little puffy," strikes me as more robust and handsome than previously described. Trotting the far side of the fairway, he stops and ponders the ground. His head tilts. "Pay close attention," Kessler whispers. "You might witness a pounce any second. Gophers and voles, that's what he wants." But the pounce never comes, and for fifteen minutes we trail Goggles at a respectful distance of fifty feet. Then he turns, glances at us—*snap-snap-snap*, goes the camera—and disappears into heavy brush.

The afternoon dimming into evening, we wander the back nine, poking about in thickets, enjoying the exploration, Kessler recounting stories as we stroll. Once she observed snoozing siblings for thirteen hours. (They stirred occasionally to harmonize with howling ambulance sirens.) Another time, determined to travel through the night with a particularly welcoming coyote, she told her husband not to worry if she wasn't home by sunrise. (The coyote ditched her earlier than expected.) She's seen about everything in the field, from coyotes that have been hit by cars to one that understood traffic signals and would wait patiently for the light to change before dashing across the street.

Eventually, inevitably, I raise the obvious question: Why? Why would a woman with no formal biological training pursue an animal that many folks consider a pest, a damn varmint, and that others say has no business living in a city?

"You get to know them," Kessler offers. "Their world

opens up, the details of their days. It's a soap opera: Wow, am I going to see that youngster again? Is his sister going to be around? Is Dad going to be aggressive with him? There's always a cliffhanger." Though she's collected scat samples for a University of California professor studying coyote DNA, has consulted with groups in Texas and Georgia that are trying to establish coexistence management plans, and is writing a book based on her coyote observations, it's this multigenerational family saga that keeps her passionate, this backyard melodrama playing out across the years. "Like with the pedal harp," she says. "You get lost in the music. It absorbs you. You become part of it and nothing else exists."

Revisiting the fairway, we're surprised by the sight of Goggles hunting exactly where we initially spotted him. This time he treats us to a number of acrobatic pounces, all unsuccessful. Kessler says that she usually departs when she can't see to shoot—*snap-snap-snap*—and both of us chuckle. If that were true, we'd have been out of here a half-hour ago.

Soon it's full-on night, and Goggles is all but gone; I can barely make him out curled up in a ball, five feet from a paved cart path. Kessler and I sit in silence, squinting into the dark, not quite ready to leave. "We could call it quits," she says. "Or, if you'd like, we could play with my night-vision goggles."

I must have misheard. Was that *night-vision goggles?*

"They're really just a toy."

She pulls what looks like a regular pair of binoculars from her backpack and hands them to me. In a flash, it's daylight again—a key-lime sort of daylight, the fairway a pale wash, Goggles a coyote-shaped splotch of ink. The per-spective is magical, like I've been sucked through a portal and granted access to a secret San Francisco.

"Here come some people," Kessler says, excited and tense. "Keep your eye on him. See what he does." I pan, and five teenage girls stroll into view. They follow the cart path, moving directly toward Goggles, oblivious. He raises his head an inch—and my chest tightens.

Four, three, two steps away: The girls are closing in, chit-chatting, near enough to notice a coyote's hot breath on their ankles if they were to shed their socks. Goggles flicks his ears and puts his chin down on the ground. He knows they don't know. He knows this is his turf, his zone. He knows there's no issue, no problem, no need to react.

The girls pass by, none the wiser, and I lower the night-vision goggles. The scene goes murky; for a moment, I'm blind.

"The only thing we're missing now is a howl," says a voice. "Then we'd have the perfect outing."

# Stucco'd All Over

I had a college professor who studied squirrels. In fact, he ate, slept, and breathed squirrels—you know the type. *Squirrel, where? Did it have grizzled-gray dorsal fur? Was it digging for ectomycorrhizal fungi? On a scale of one to ten, was it an eleven?*

Specifically, this professor adored the tassel-eared—or Abert's—squirrel, a denizen of the Rocky Mountains' cool, dry ponderosa pine forests. As the name suggests, the species's distinguishing morphological characteristic is a tuft of hair extending approximately three centimeters from each ear. "Truly elegant," wrote naturalist S. W. Woodhouse in 1853.

But here's the interesting thing—my professor, the Squirrel Man, also had hairy ears. That's right, the dude was tufted, tasseled, truly elegant. Furthermore, he boasted an impressive beard, a pelage really, and drank coffee in such quantities that during lectures he climbed the classroom walls. I've never met a person who so resembled, in both physical form and spirit, a member of the genus *Sciurus*.

Which raises the question: Do wildlife lovers assume qualities of the beloved? Put another way: Does the very act of sustained observation lead to a transformation of our bodies and minds?

This may sound ridiculous, but it's not. Consider the devoted marine biologist swimming in endless pursuit of some sleek, streamlined fish. After hundreds of hours in the water, won't certain of her muscles have developed and others atrophied? Or take the diehard ornithologist roaming inky-dark woodlands, searching for owls. It seems likely that she will eventually develop superior night vision, doesn't it?

Another professor of mine, a guy who ate, slept, and breathed Plato, summed up the ancient Greek understanding of psychology with the line, "You become like the object you intend." It's a fancy way of saying that the things we spend time with, commit our senses to, and reflect on do indeed alter us. The *Stanford Encyclopedia of Philosophy* defines intentionality as the power of minds to be *about* something. If your mind is entirely about, say, a prairie dog or a salamander, where does that leave the so-called *you*?

Walt Whitman touches on this perplexing logic when he describes himself as "stucco'd with quadrupeds and birds all over." That's quite the image—a human plastered with bits and pieces of other creatures, zoologically collaged both inside and out. How does the poet, or for that matter the naturalist, hybridize with his animal neighbors? Whitman provides an answer a few stanzas later: "I stand and look at them long and long."

Cut to a small park in San Francisco ringed with Monterey pines where, more often than not, yours truly can be found looking long and long at a family of red-tailed hawks. I located their nest a month ago—airborne feces and my stucco'd baseball cap facilitated the discovery—and have been visiting regularly ever since. To stare. To study. To jot notes.

Actually, that last part is a lie. Halfway through my third marathon session with the hawks, I dropped my pencil and didn't bend to pick it up. Somehow, paying close attention to these birds turns off the intellectual, analytical region of my brain. Just being nearby, splitting the difference between meditation and mesmerization, constitutes my method of inquiry.

A couple centuries before Whitman, the haiku master Bashō, a Zen Buddhist, entreated his disciples, "Go to the pine if you want to learn about the pine, or to the bamboo if you want to learn about the bamboo. And in doing so, you must leave your subjective preoccupation with yourself. Otherwise you impose yourself on the object and do not learn." I'm a few notches shy of enlightenment, but this does jibe with my daily practice in the park.

I stand long and long. I look longer and longer. The tunnel of my binoculars, by focusing consciousness, makes me *about* that nest of awkward, tottering, almost-fledged juveniles. They turn their heads, scanning for mother and father, and I do the same, my eyes in a squint. A chilly gust ruffles their feathers, sneaks under my collar, and we all shy away, hunching into ourselves for warmth. Everybody spaces out. Borders blur. I slide toward the edge of me and the beginning of them.

And then, so fast, the raptors are dancing a jig and I'm dancing a jig and the air is full of cries because Mom's coming in hot with a mouse. Dinner is served!

Perhaps this is getting too wacky. Let's grab hold of

something solid, something tangible—for instance, Squirrel Man's ears. Are they the result of his decades-long fascination with *Sciurus aberti*? No, probably not. I'll be the first
to admit that those magnificent tufts of his are beyond my
ken. Honestly, this entire subject, though exciting, leaves
me a tad dizzy.

But just in case there is some truth here—just in case the
lover of wildlife does assume qualities of the beloved—why
not offer a quick word of encouragement to the passionate
folks who research blobfishes, monkfishes, walruses, matamata turtles, vampire bats, and naked mole rats? I say be
not deterred. I say follow your heart's idiosyncratic path.
On a scale of one to ten, you freaks are an eleven. Pay no
attention to the haters, the superficial haters, when they call
you ugly.

# *Birdnap*

The story begins in Arizona, when I was working as a bio-logical science technician on a northern goshawk demog-raphy study. My job involved identifying banded birds, and that meant rising at dawn, hanging around nest areas, waiting for a prey delivery. Often I'd scope an elusive male's anklet by eight a.m., then recline in the duff at the foot of a ponderosa pine for a couple minutes of shut-eye. Once or twice, maybe three times, I woke with a start to the surreal vision of a raptor perched on a nearby branch, its crimson eyes lasering me.

*Whoa. Is this a dream?*

It wasn't long before I realized that napping with birds could be its own pastime, an enriching practice to deliber-ately pursue with different species in different habitats.

Since leaving Arizona, I've conked off with golden eagles on Colorado's fourteen-thousand-foot peaks, trumpeter swans at Montana's Red Rock Lakes, Costa's hummingbirds in the Mojave, and ravens gossiping above the Hoh Rainfor-est's dense green canopy—not to mention owls, from the great horned to the flammulated. The bulk of my avian doz-ing, however, has taken place in the Bay Area: Goat Rock to Point Reyes, Pescadero to the Golden Gate. San Francisco's overgrown corners make for fantastic urban birdnapping (nuthatches weave blankets of twittering all through the summer afternoons!), and even riding the Amtrak east from Richmond there are avocets and egrets on mudflats beyond the pillow-window.

Normally we conceive of birding as a senses-on-high-alert activity: Only she who is vigilant, *fully awake*, will catch the flash of scapulars there in the tangled woods. Well, sure, I've been known to gulp a pot of black coffee and eagerly apply myself to scanning, scanning, scanning, David Allen Sibley and Roger Tory Peterson spurring me on. But there's also something to be said for attention's opposite, isn't there? For relaxing? For easing ourselves into a different relationship with warblers and thrushes, pelicans and grebes?

What it comes down to is the liminal mode, the edge-of-unconscious state of being, the twilighty threshold. Sometimes a winter wren's mad crackly song mixes with babbling human voices rising from the depths of my psyche. Sometimes sandhill cranes visit me, pausing for a second—or an hour, or a season—to rest on the flooded fields of my insides. Sometimes (as with the goshawk work) I wake groggy, confused, and there's a predatory monster, blood on the curved beak, so close.

*Am I still asleep? Does it even matter?*

An admittedly odd activity, yes, but that's not to say oneiric ornithology (*oneiros* is the Greek word for "dream") lacks sympathetic friends. As a motto or mission statement, I borrow the following from Nan Shepherd, a Scottish author who was devoted to experiencing the Cairngorms, her chosen range, via every possible angle: "No one knows the mountain completely who has not slept on it. As one slips over into sleep, the mind grows limpid; the body melts; perception alone remains. These moments of quiescent perceptiveness before sleep are among the most rewarding of the day. I am emptied of preoccupation, there is nothing between me and the earth and sky."

Birdnapping is special for countless reasons: It invites a prolonged engagement with particular beds (forests, meadows, those overgrown corners of San Francisco, etc.); it counterbalances the rush-go-strive mentality that in our culture too often infects purportedly "chill" hobbies; and it embraces everybody from the tired toddler to the somnolent senior by deemphasizing the importance of skill and expertise. If I had to choose one single aspect to celebrate, though, it would definitely be Shepherd's "nothing between me and," her notion of the discerning, objectifying, separating intellect dissolving away so that a new appreciation of connectivity can emerge.

Which reminds me of another quote, this from Robert Aitken, the late Hawaiian writer and Zen priest who I suspect would have enjoyed the playful adventure of a nap with his local mynahs and waxbills: "Drowsy contentment may be a condition close to realization. It is a kind of emptiness, of nondifferentiation, where the ten directions melt: inside and outside become one."

*Wait a second*, you might be thinking. *Did this kooky guy just liken Buddhist enlightenment to yawning with the aves?* Fair enough. It's probably time for a scene, an anecdote to return my highfalutin theorizing back to earth.

April. The Sonoma coast. Toes sifting sand. I'd been pan-

ning with binos most of the morning, picking surf scoters
out of curling green waves, teasing pelagic cormorants from
the glinting, sun-struck Pacific. Squinting hard, I spotted a
wavering line about half a mile from the shore, so faint as to
be nearly invisible. With considerable tuning of the focus
and furrowing of my brow, the line eventually resolved into
a fluid chain of birds, hundreds of them, bill to tail to bill to
tail to bill to tail. Pacific loons? A tingle zipped the length
of my spine. Pacific loons migrating south from Alaska! I
hadn't identified this species in the field before. In my life
as a conventional birder, it was a personal achievement, a
distinct satisfaction.

I watched until my brain hurt, fifteen or twenty minutes,
then took a break to ponder. Regardless of whether I spotted them, those loons would be out there, tracing the coast,
pushing south at the limit of sight. How much is flying past
us all the time? How many of nature's thrilling spectacles
are we missing? A lot is missed because we fail to look,
because we fail to pay attention. But perhaps a lot more is
missed because we look too hard, because we avoid that
edge, that border where the noticing takes on an entirely
different quality. Says the narrator (a natural historian)
in a short story by Barry Lopez: "I developed methods of
inquiry, although I appeared to be doing nothing....I appeared completely detached....I appeared to be asleep. But
I was not."

Tucking the binos into their case, I settled my head
against the beach, welcoming that wild spectacle—that
flow of feathers along the continent's margin—to pass
through the part of me I do not own, control, understand, or
need to understand. And when I woke a while later, having

dreamed something powerful, something important, some-thing that was made of parts but moved as one, something that was ultimately old and yet ultimately new, something I couldn't quite remember, couldn't quite name—there it was. Still flowing. A wavering line connecting the faraway to the now, the here.

# The Anthropological Aesthetic

Over the past couple of months, I have galloped across Comancheria with the Texas Rangers, discovered lost Epicurean manuscripts in the company of the Renaissance humanist Poggio Bracciolini, and contemplated the cloud-reflecting Yangtze alongside ancient Chinese poets. I am an omnivorous bibliophile—sonnets, satires, you name it. So long as the words sing to the heart and the lines click together in the mind like puzzle pieces—so long as it's "good" writing, painstakingly fashioned to generate some intellectual-emotional movement within me—I'll read and read, regardless of subject.

Strange, then, given this appreciation of literary artistry, that the best book I've encountered in some time is a monotonous, encyclopedia-style academic text originally published in 1933 as part of the decidedly obscure Bulletin of Milwaukee Public Museum series. *Miwok Material Culture: Indian Life of the Yosemite Region,* written by a pair of University of California anthropologists and based on interviews with "Native informants," should be a total snooze. Outside of a few ivory tower–dwellers, primitive-skills enthusiasts, and families descended from Miwok stock, who cares that a decoction of skullcap was utilized as a wash for sore eyes?

Or that acorn mush was deemed "insipid" without an accompaniment of seed meal? Or that the Plains, Southern, Central, and Northern dialect groups each had their own unique terms for the twined burden basket?

Turns out that I care, intensely, and if you're an omnivorous bibliophile, that's big news. There's a certain aesthetic at work in *Miwok*, what I've taken to calling the Anthropological Aesthetic. This is über-nonfiction, nonfiction that goes so far into reality it becomes a subspecies of art, a poem-myth about methods, knowledges, possibilities. Not merely beautiful—it's useful.

I don't want to oversimplify things by saying that the American Empire is collapsing, dragging much of nature down with it, but I can't deny that, looking around, absorbing the news and the sights, it often feels as though *I'm* falling. What to reach for? Melville? Tolstoy? *Vanity Fair*? *Calvin and Hobbes*? How about a book that gazes forward and backward at the same time? To borrow a phrase from the late Arizona writer Charles Bowden: "memories of the future."

~

I found *Miwok* at a yard sale three years ago and bought it for a dime, mostly because the cover—a black-and-white photograph from 1880 of two painted, deadpan, headdress-wearing fellows—was intriguing and a little spooky. Over the past handful of summers, I've explored what previously was the core of the Sierra Miwok's territory (a swath of "Gold Country" running from Mariposa in the south to Placerville in the north), but I never intended to formally study the landscape or its residents. The book was one more volume on a crowded shelf, that's all.

Last winter, needing something to browse at the breakfast table—and why not something with pictures of obsidian blades, deer-bone awls, soaproot brushes, willow cradles, and dance skirts made of magpie feathers?—I gave *Miwok* a try. To my surprise, I was swiftly transported to a vivid world, one that sprang from the empty spaces *between* the dusty facts.

Women wearing hides chatted as they milled nuts in a bedrock mortar, coppery sunlight on their bare shoulders. An entire hungry village circled a meadow for a grasshopper drive, beating the insects toward pits and smudge fires. A hundred pairs of hands worked sinew and milkweed fiber and grapevine withes and steatite and soil, crafting from raw earth—from nothing *but* raw earth—a richly nuanced way of life.

Manzanita cider.

Walnut dice games.

Shamans shaking butterfly-cocoon rattles.

By the time I finally made it from the breakfast table to the couch, I was hooked, my plans for the day shot. Come evening, the book was finished and I was exhausted, most every page dog-eared and exuberantly underlined.

~

Wanting to better understand the word-magic of the Anthropological Aesthetic, I picked *Miwok* up recently and reread it, cover to cover. As with the fantasy and sci-fi stories that captivated me as a kid, for the bulk of twenty-four hours I inhabited an alternate reality. But here's the wondrous thing—it's a *real* reality, not a make-believe realm. Visiting the quarry at Lotowayaka, observing the tattooing of an adolescent girl, these allow for the most expansive, important, and enlivening thought a person can think: There are other ways to live, to be. Our way right now, with its glowing screens and nature-deficit disorder, its drone strikes and La-Z-Boys, its Republicans and Democrats, its dollars and distraction, is not the *only* way. That may seem obvious, but it's depressingly easy—and dangerous—to forget.

Other ways? To live? To be? Sweet blessed breath of fresh air and perspective! *Miwok* provides what Malcolm Margolin, publisher of the magazine *News from Native California*, has described as "glimpses of almost forgotten aspects of our own selves."

Still, the question remains: How does a basic text—not a masterfully told narrative or entertaining yarn—cast such a compelling spell? The answer lies, I think, in another quote, this from the Montana writer William Kittredge: "Listings are attempts to make existence whole and holy in the naming."

The no-frills *Miwok*—essentially a 150-page ladder of paragraphs with rungs labeled "Salt," "Ear and Nose Piercing," and "Dogs," to mention but a few—is surely meant to be consulted, not read straight through. When we do read it page by page, though, its thousands of super-specific details create a pattern of daily life, of cycling seasons, of humans in place. This survey of material culture isn't limited to tools and ornaments; it encompasses everything from the proper technique for harvesting *Pinus sabiniana*'s cones (twist them off when they're green), to how people should treat their hair during a period of mourning (cut it and bury the locks beside the deceased). There's a hypnotic, incantatory quality to the relentless iterations: X was stone-boiled or roasted in ashes, whereas Y was exclusively boiled, whereas Z was parched, pounded, and eaten dry.

On the other hand, what this survey of material culture omits (in addition to characters, plot, and similar devices) is any commentary on the *meaning* of the artifacts and techniques documented. I've come to believe that this absence of interpretation—this vacuum around the bare, skeletal facts—is actually integral to the functioning of the Anthropological Aesthetic.

George Saunders, the lauded contemporary fiction writer, says he aggressively cuts from his stories so that readers are forced to fill in the gaps and engage. In *Miwok*, the novelist's imperative "show, don't tell" is pushed to an extreme. For example, the section "Taking of Fishes" offers a tantalizing reference to rainbow trout "caught by hand in the holes along the banks of creeks and rivers." That's it. No thoughts. No daydreams. No hint of interior life, of a real individual standing motionless in cold water, performing what most of us today consider an impossible task.

Critics might accuse a book like this of draining a culture's vitality by presenting its flutes instead of its tunes, its bead necklaces minus the ceremonies they adorned. But this spare treatment is precisely what can spark a whole and holy existence in the imagination. How does it feel to stare for hours into a swirling eddy, waiting for a shadowy piscine flicker? And what is it like to snap awake, the trance of focus broken, a rainbow trout glittering in your fist? To find out, *Miwok* insists, we must wade into the current ourselves.

~

As mentioned earlier, the highest pleasure of reading is, for me, a synchronized movement of the intellect *and* the emotions. The epiphany of "other ways" is primarily mental. What of that red muscle pulsing inside the chest?

In the introductory pages of *Miwok,* a truth most of us would rather avoid forces itself upon the heart with words like "disrupted," "impacted," "depleted," "vanished." Of the numerous California tribes displaced and decimated by white settlers and soldiers, we learn that the Sierra Miwok were arguably "the greatest sufferers because the principal gold-bearing regions lay in their territory." It's a familiar story, one of intricately textured inhabitation and catastrophic violence. *Miwok* doesn't tell it outright, moving briskly to the fire drills and arrow straighteners and coyote-skin pillows, but nonetheless the story haunts the margins of each page.

I encountered this very ghost during a June backpacking trip in the Stanislaus National Forest, on the Sierra's western slope: Douglas firs, granite outcrops, northern flickers galore. Back in the day, these ridges and valleys were also home to an animal called *Homo sapiens.* Now the land is a federally protected wilderness area where a guy needs a permit to walk and sleep. Times change, as they say. And cultures, for sometimes ghastly reasons, disappear.

On that trip, there were moments charging uphill when I felt as if my heart would explode. It's just the exercise, I told myself, just the cardio. But then, hitting some incredible vista, I'd want to both weep and laugh: for the beauty of the land, for the sadness of the land, for the memory—which is the *future possibility*—of humankind living on and with and as a part of the land. At those moments, I pulled out a certain dog-eared, exuberantly underlined book, took a seat, and read a page at random.

Brush assembly house.

Digging stick.

Warriors in grass caps.

Thank you, I said aloud, remembering that morning at the breakfast table, the cover falling open to reveal a whole and holy world I didn't yet know that I badly needed to read, and read again, and keep reading.

Snowberry.

Moccasin.

Grizzly bear.

Thank you, I said, standing up, shouldering my pack, pushing deeper into the range—into that world and this world and the next world, all at once.

# Thoughts after an Owl

Yesterday, wandering at dusk in the brown hills that rise from this condo-sprawl called Palm Springs, California, I spent half an hour with a long-eared owl. I tell you most sincerely that there are few creatures as stirringly strange and spookily stirring and mystically mystical as birds from the order *Strigiformes*. Very much the griffin of legend, these birds—that is if the griffin of legend upped its weirdness by a factor of 15.

Dinosaur feet. Shaggy sheep legs. A body of feathers and fur and leaves and twigs and shattered bits of light and shadow. Of course, the face is part human, part cat, part seal, and affixed to a head that seemingly twists 360 degrees. If that's not enough, this vision, this being, this power, my how it launches into the air and glides silently on—no, can't be possible—on forty inches of wing!

I hate to make a bold statement (hyperbole, my nemesis, my temptress), but it feels more and more that every single time I go outdoors I am buckling up for a borderline hallucinatory experience. The natural world just does not fail to provoke in me awe, wonder, vibes of fear, tingles of trepidation, and a kind of meditative drift-state wherein all the senses knit all their sense-data together to form a kind of synesthetic carpet, a magic rug on which I sail off to who knows where. Did I tell you about the desert blister beetles I met recently, *Lytta magister* in nasty gooey sexed-up swarms? As Harvey, my old jolly antique-tractor-collecting neighbor from childhood in Vermont would say, *Sheeeit.* To spend ten minutes with these beetles, *sheeeit*, you better be buckled, maybe even helmeted.

A week ago, hiking solo in that same dessicated, rugged, so-brown labyrinth of hills, that topographic maze flanking the Palm Springs shitstrip (sheeeitstrip) of megachurches, payday loan pawnshops, car dealerships, windborne litter, bearded men masticated by a brutal economic system and subsequently regurgitated onto the street with only junk-filled shopping carts to call home—hiking solo in them thar wacky hills, I couldn't even put my hand down to touch things, like curious rock-things or plant-things or stick-things.

The reason I couldn't touch, say, a funky stick that drew my attention, and that a part of me did badly want to touch, was because my hand, my flesh, my integument, was scared to do so. It was like these hands, which are so friggin' sensitive, would gather too, too, too much information, too, too, too much vital presence and place-specific truth. My feet were sheltered by leather, soled with rubber. My body *needed* that mediation. The hands, though, were and are naked, literally naked, naked nonstop.

It's interesting, don't you agree? We all recognize that if you show up at work buckass birthday-suit nude, the entire experience will get awkward, intense. Pause here. Consider. That's what your hands do each day! They live *outside*, with nothing to hide behind. Bushwhacking around last week, as mentioned, was odd indeed: I was nervous to even lay a wee digit on this dry freaky earth.

Granted, there was probably one more thing at play, which is the prickliness and poisonousness of the desert, the possibility of camouflaged snakes and spiders and scorpions and whatnot (the equivalent in the mossy green Vermont of my youth would be putting your hand down on an obese slug, a rotting possum, a sodden deer carcass). And that right there loops to my initial point regarding the nearly hallucinatory quality of a simple, routine, back-of-the-sheeeitstrip-at-dusk walk: Any moment it can feel like some griffin or mystical face is about to pop out and zap you with huge yellow eyes. It can feel like a stick beneath your hand might not be a stick but rather the body of a serpent, or a mass of writhing ants, or some small somebody who has a soul and a voice and will speak across the self/other boundary. It can feel like you might be encountering—the divine?

Once, camping on and with a blocky Colorado mountain, heart of winter, blue moonlight washing over snow, me sitting in that snow, no tent, no plan, just sitting there in the middle of the clear-cold night's vast crystalline silence, a fox pawed up within five feet, looked me in the eye, hung out, swung its tail, then walked away. I will repeat that: A blue moony fox faced my face, eyed my eye, hung *out*, came rushing *in* (the sparking electric current of unadulterated perception!), then walked away.

Godspeed.

# NEVADA

# Somewhere in the Middle of Nowhere

There is no road, hasn't been a road since Gerlach, that crust of a town where we turned from pavement to playa, to hairline-fractured hardpan, and the truck transcended its truckness to become one with the earth. Dust swings left and right in the rearview mirror, a brown tail whipping into oblivion the memories of Reno's traffic and Fernley's crowded Walmart parking lot. The dust erases and welcomes. The dust coats tongues. Ancient Lake Lahontan's parched floor is at once beneath our tires and in the air.

The four of us—childhood friends from Vermont, high school brothers scattered to various corners of the country, so-called grown men—don't give a fat flying hoot about next month's Burning Man festivities. We've pilgrimaged to Nevada's Black Rock Desert not for sixty thousand humans, not for lasers and *womp-womp* bass and skyscraper flames, but for the desert's own severe weirdness. Its isolation. Its fierce summer heat. Specifically, we're interested in the trailless maze, the jumbled volcanic mess, that is King Lear Peak's west slope.

Sweat out the sins of a well-lived life, says somebody, raising a toast to tomorrow's climb.

*Click, click, click*—the chorus of beer cans. Amen, amen, amen.

Last time the gang got together was Arizona, the Grand Canyon, that hungry hugeness so famous for eating eons and hours and everything between, including the name you carry to its rim, drop like a pebble, kiss goodbye. Maybe that kiss is why, without fail, we choose the arid West's skeleton landscapes for these reunion trips? To abandon ourselves? To serve ourselves raw to the raw terrain? Maybe that's the urge behind the drinking too?

We wonder and wander and laugh the truck onto a rugged two-track that leads to sagebrush, sagebrush, sagebrush, and eventually a Bureau of Land Management sign, its map peppered with bullet holes. Pissing for just shy of eternity, I read the toponyms of nowhere's middle: Old Razorback Mountain, Mormon Dan Butte, Lassen-Clapper Murder Site, Sawtooth Knob. Then it's more speed, more cranium-scouring scenery, the Jackson Mountains rising wall-like, King Lear's craggy crown piercing the blue sky at 8,923 feet.

A jackrabbit darts, stops, darts.

Excuse me, sir, madam, might we park here?

Out come the coolers for seats and out goes our attention, eight eyes scanning desolation. We make like the dust and settle, kick off the sandals and relax. Mustangs pass far to the north of camp, their heads lowered. One with a white mane ghosts away from the herd.

Wild horses? Spirits of the desiccated void? Emissaries from the place past all places? Living on what? Living how? It's a slow, dreamy kind of surprise, the brain's movements hardly noticeable against such vastness. We hand binoculars back and forth, back and forth.

No green, mossy, Vermont-born soul could ever feel at home in this wasteland, says somebody.

*Click, click, click*—the chorus.

As planned, and without the slightest effort, the afternoon becomes a pile of cans, which in turn becomes a red sinking sun, which in turn becomes a half-dozen nighthawks winging low and fast and sharp in pursuit of insects. The insects become feathers, become blood, and keep flying in their new form. It all happens right in front of us, unobscured. The purple dusk becomes a moon-sliver, the moonsliver a slurred run of jokes, the jokes a stumble toward bed.

Lying supine, sleeping bags rolled out, consciousness easing into its rest, a massive whispering darkness fills the ears: *Middle of nowhere, middle of nowhere, middle of…*

But that phrase, it's wrong, isn't it?

After our long day of travel and awe, after celebrating the myths of dead emptiness and places past all places, we're starting to sort of understand. The jackrabbits, the mustangs, the nighthawks—the history held in names like Mormon Dan, in bullet holes, in the sediments of ancient Lake Lahontan—these all proclaim the same truth. That nowhere is the middle of nowhere. That everywhere is the middle of somewhere. That nature has no edges. That the center is relentlessly here, now, as it is back in the Green Mountains of our youth, south at the Grand Canyon, in Gerlach, in Fernley's Walmart parking lot, in Reno, wherever.

Tomorrow, yes, tomorrow we'll wake before dawn, drag ass up the broken ridges and chossy gullies in soft pink light, scrape our fingers against the undeniable reality of this land. By noon, if things go smoothly, if nobody pukes from exhaustion, we'll stand atop the summit of King Lear, hearts ticking in our chapped lips and drumming in our temples, jaws slack.

Or we won't. Perhaps we'll just hunker, curl under the truck and nap in its meager shade. Having come this far, it hardly matters.

Countless stars are spinning overhead, chasing one another in dizzying circles. Either the drink has finally caught us or this patch of desert, this pinprick, this speck of a speck, this actually is the center of the universe, the axis on which the cosmos rotates.

Amen, says somebody, probably a jackrabbit.

Amen.

# Listening to Big Empty

I wake at dawn, and before my eyes even open, I'm drenched by the creek. Not the water but the song, the liquid harmony braiding and unbraiding ten feet beyond the tent's thin wall. No need for the blindfold yet, I tell myself. Stay warm in the sleeping bag, listening to this music.

The coffee ritual gets me, though, and soon I'm at the picnic table, firing up the stove, hearing the hiss of propane, the grinding flick of a lighter. For a while there's just my boots stomping heat into numb toes, the odd dark-eyed junco clicking in snowy underbrush. Then it's the percolator's oh-so-sweet gurgle and a deliciously bitter sip that pricks my ears.

Getting here, to this day of uninterrupted focus, was a chore—six hours of tires whumping over old pavement, six hours of pop-country and ranting talk show hosts. Great Basin National Park is located south of Route 50 in Nevada, the nation's so-called Loneliest Road. Since 1934 the park has welcomed a total of 3.5 million visitors, which is about how many people flooded Zion National Park's sandstone canyons in 2015 alone. Where better than the Big Empty to practice walking the land with ears in your feet?

Actually, the plan isn't to walk—that proves tricky once

blindfolded—but to sit. To explore the uncharted microto-pography of snaps, grumbles, chirrs, buzzes, and burbles. To stage a quiet revolt against the tyranny of eyesight, the dominant and mostly unquestioned belief in our culture that nature is primarily a visual spectacle.

Years ago in Grand Teton National Park, on what had to be the most postcard-perfect autumn weekend of all eternity, I tied a bandanna around my head—blacked out the vistas, deposed the tyrant. My friends were incredulous: Why conduct your little sensory deprivation experiment now, in the presence of these stupendously toothy peaks? I told them that it wasn't deprivation I was after, but the opposite. Enrichment. A nuanced sense of the terrain. A hidden park inside the park.

At that exact moment, or so the story goes in my memory, a bull elk bugled nearby, sending overtones rushing through the forest. Countless aspen leaves rattled on their stems. The bones in my body whistled like so many flutes. For an instant that felt more like an hour, nobody made a peep.

See, I said.

Then I quickly corrected myself, cinching the blindfold tighter: *Hear.*

~

That nature is more than scenes and scenery, more than a movie to watch or some image to capture and upload, is hardly a new thought. George Catlin, the frontier painter who in 1832 proposed "a nation's Park," included in his vision (excuse that sneaky ocular metaphor) a prairie refuge characterized by "desolate fields of silence." John Muir could supposedly identify every tree species in the Sierra Nevada simply by listening to its "wind-music."

Natural sounds don't just provide listeners with a sense of place—they *are* the place, no less than dirt and grizzly bears. Wilderness fragmented by human din is not wild, and an ecosystem gone mute won't function as it should. Frogs need to discuss potential dangers. Birds need to court by crooning. Quite simply, land conservation, to deserve the name, must include the conservation of soundscapes.

The National Park Service picked up on this in 1972 when the Noise Control Act was passed, a law requiring the federal government to regulate, among other things, commercial helicopter and airplane tours over national parks. But it wasn't until 2000, with the creation of a natural sounds division, that the agency got serious about "protecting, maintaining, and restoring acoustical environments." Tasks range from baseline audio sampling at frontcountry and backcountry sites to the analysis of burgeoning threats, such as growing crowds and industrial development adjacent to park boundaries.

Intrusive anthropogenic noise, while a serious issue, is but half the problem. The other half is underhearing. Disregard. Earbuds. A negligence on the part of hikers and picnickers and photographers to open themselves to potential opportunities. Can we climb El Capitan's immaculate granite with our ears? Can we watch a Yellowstone wolf's howl cut across the face of the full moon without ever lifting our gaze? These whimsical questions should be asked and answered by experts and regular parkgoers alike. They should be engaged with playfully, in the field.

As pioneering soundscape ecologist Bernie Krause puts it, writing of the Grand Canyon: "The pictures of the park really do only convey a fraction of the experience." If you're not *hearing* the ancient stratigraphy crumbling grain by grain, you might as well be sitting on the tour bus, looking out the window.

~

After a strong cup of coffee and twenty minutes of keen listening—the juncos, I realize, have taken to the pinyon pines, their voices mapping in my mind the precise location of perches—an annoying rumble rises in my gut. Nope, not hunger. The *other* morning rumble, the one that follows a dinner of baked beans, hotdogs, and beer. Like a rockfall in the echoey alpine cirque of my belly.

Strolling to the bathroom, I work on parsing the various sounds within a single footstep: the crush of loose surface snow, then the creak as the sole flexes and compacts the base, and last the tinkle of crystals thrown ahead by the push-off. It's November, a squall forecasted to arrive this morning, and the campground is vacant—not that I would expect otherwise. On my first trip here, I climbed 13,065-foot Wheeler Peak, the park's centerpiece, and had the entire summit to myself. Plus a sizable chunk of the Great Basin. Plus the whining of my nervous system, the pulse of blood in my temples.

Today I'm hoping to hear nothing, or almost nothing. The approaching storm's invisible edge. My small fidgeting within the heave and sigh of some larger elemental calm. It's hard to describe the way our world knits itself into wholeness one whir and rustle at a time without getting all cheesy and metaphysical, but it's true, very real.

A Clark's nutcracker cuts by with a whoosh of wings, arresting me midstep, and the sky audibly regathers itself in the bird's wake. Then the spell's gone, dissolved, which is a good thing, as it would be dangerous to delay my rendezvous with the "comfort station" any longer.

Misnomer? You bet your frigid fanny, and you can throw in the icy seat as well! Never fear, I'm a pretty tough guy, and moreover, I'm beginning to get lost in aural reveries. I experiment with the concrete walls and the ping-ponging resonance, humming for a few minutes, chanting some bass notes. Boy, if I could get a corvid in here, I think, then we'd really be jamming.

Back outside, the mountain slope above the campground is beginning to moan, a lenticular cloud forming around Wheeler Peak's summit. Channeling Muir, I hike into the pinyon-juniper woodlands—pausing, crouching, trying to distinguish between the thrum of sagebrush and the thrum of cliffrose. Identities emerge. Mormon tea is whispery, delicate. Mountain mahogany is coarse, gruff. Prickly pears have little to say, though they do nip at the ear when I lean in too close. I'm reminded of other natural history pursuits—sorting seashells, parsing lichens with a hand lens—and how the ecological community starts to resemble just that: a community, a neighborhood of individuals.

The nondescript forest is suddenly described. A snag and a living tree speak the same language but different dialects. Even the growing wind comes across as a gang of many.

～

Far as I can tell, the sounds we absorb—a mountain lion's scream, a glacier's groan—become landmarks in our personal sonic geography. Capitol Reef National Park is for

me the back-and-forth of raven chortles inside slickrock alcoves. Rocky Mountain National Park is an electric crackle
and the slam of thunder against an exposed ridgeline. Of a
solo backpacking trip on the beaches of the Olympic Peninsula, the color I remember is gray—foggy gray, continu-
ous gray. But the push and rake of waves, that was strange,
unforgettable. By day the ocean laughed like a schoolyard
of happy children. By night it bellowed like a tortured monster. And it never stopped. It was always speaking, even
when it wasn't.

Hiking along, I ruminate. Maybe it's not so much *what*
we hear as that we *attempt* to hear, that occasionally we
meet a landscape delicately, on tiptoes, alert to possibilities. Maybe it's this effort and intention that drops a pin
flag into our life. Maybe park rangers should hand out com-
plimentary blindfolds as a way of encouraging toddlers
and grandparents and everybody else to take it easy, quit
the chitchat. Maybe once our ears are tuned, once the practice has been ingrained, we can abandon the blindfolds and
enjoy a synesthetic wonderland, our senses working in con-
cert to perceive an infinitely layered world.

Maybe, maybe. Not today.

After a few slow miles, a soughing draws me to a particular pinyon pine. I lie down in a crunchy patch of exposed
duff on the leeward side of the trunk, bark inches from my
forehead. Out comes a thick cotton bandanna, soft on the
bridge of my nose.

Stories unfold beneath the pine, all without beginning,
middle, or end, all without plot or character. Branches clat-
ter against branches. A million needles sift fast-moving air.
I want to rip free the bandanna, find the source of a specific

sound, but the fun is hanging in there, riding the ride, letting the tension build. Sometimes the wind is too intense, like an eighteen-wheeler is about to smash me into oblivion. I brace for impact, tensing every muscle, only to relax seconds later—ah, an unexpected lull.

Bernie Krause again: "When the sound of wind is hushed and subtle, it sometimes reminds me of the breath of living organisms; it becomes the crossover between animals and an alive-sounding earth."

This is my last thought before thinking stops altogether, before I disappear. Where do I go? Away, that's all I can say. I travel, return, separate from a state of consciousness that resembles dreaming yet involves no slumber. Pulling off the blindfold, I try to stand but stumble instead. I can barely see, barely walk, barely pick up the journal that falls from my pocket—and when I do, there are no notes to write.

Words fail. The day's eloquence presses against me from all sides. I'm out of it. By which I mean in it. Way deep.

And then I'm in my jacket's hood, the storm's first snowflakes scratching tiny poems—haiku—against the nylon.

❦   ❦   ❦

# WYOMING

# The Irrigator's Club

A friend in Wyoming wrote me, saying one guy quit the ranch and they could use a sub. Okay, why not. It was summer, and my laptop was fast becoming an enemy of all things fresh, outdoorsy, healthy, and inspired. I stowed the cursed machine, drove across two and a half states, suited up in beat jeans and leaky waders, got to work.

About that work. Flood irrigating is a dirty job, a boring job, a thankless job. Grow grass to grow cattle to grow humans. Dam ditches. Shunt water left and right. Six days a week you're in the fields at sunup, sloshing around, heaving on tarps, taking your crowbar to a recalcitrant piece of plywood jammed tight in some culvert. Maybe your four-wheeler breaks down three miles from the barn. Maybe you splinter a thumb. Maybe you run out of smokes.

And there's the shit, of course. Grow grass to grow cattle to make shit, you think, not exactly chuckling at the joke, not exactly confident, after another nine-hour shift, that it *is* a joke. For the hundredth time you step in a mushy pile. For the thousandth time. You're an irrigator. Welcome to the club.

Don't get me wrong, though—flood irrigating is also a job of texture and rhythm, big skies and deep surprises.

Black bears among cottonwoods. Elk snorting and bugling. The ranch is wild, and any morning you might see two bald eagles, a prairie falcon, a great blue heron, a yellow warbler, some seven hundred Canada geese. You might see a coyote pup. You might see a curious frog. You might encounter the real world, the elemental world, the world your laptop only offers in pretend. On rare occasions, if you're lucky, you just might *feel* it too.

I did, during my third week. Massive field. Sweaty afternoon. Sort of dazed, sort of tired, sort of happy in that dazed-tired way that doesn't register as happiness until later, when you're cracking a beer on the porch at dusk. I hopped off my wheeler and headed for a cluster of aspens on the far side of a barbed-wire fence. Ah, nothing like a lunch of peanut butter sandwiches and trembling shade.

But about fifty paces out—what the heck? I stopped, squinted. Hanging from the fence's top strand was a brown shape, a brown strangeness, a brown question mark. A paper bag pinned there by wind? A desiccated cow pie posted as a joke?

Surely you're familiar with this floaty moment between knowing and not-knowing, this drifty moment between certainty and uncertainty. Or perhaps it's more of a slide, a smooth, slow, subtle slide from pure perception—without name, without thought—to the earth's nouns, every weird vision landed in its proper place by the categorizing brain. Such confused openness never lasts long, but it renders time meaningless, so what's the difference? Oh, to be in limbo, approaching on silent feet, with silent breath, a fence you've passed repeatedly but never really noticed. Oh, to inch toward that regular humdrum fence as if it were a bomb, a god, a force.

Turns out the mystery-thing was all of the above. Crazy yellow eyes. Curved beak pasted with dried blood and torn bits of feather. A long-eared owl, caught by a barb, dangling from the thin flesh of its back. Wings spread. Alive. Assuming the collision occurred at dawn, the owl had been exposed to the baking sun for ten straight hours. Not good, I thought, coming in close, retreating, coming in close again. Clock is ticking. How to help?

With pliers I cut free a section of the fence, the depleted, desperate bird struggling to fly from this nightmare of daylight and pain and humankind, struggling to turn and bite the metal on her spine. With my shirt I wrapped the depleted, desperate bird and set her gently in the plastic crate strapped to the wheeler's hood, set her there along with the five feet of fence that wouldn't release. With softness in my voice I entreated the depleted, desperate bird—hold on, little buddy, hold on, little pal, hold on.

But she couldn't. That evening, at a raptor rehab center, she was euthanized. Just as the season had to roll forward and the nights had to lengthen and eventually the grass had to stop growing—which meant the work was through—the owl had to let go. Come September, I took off my beat jeans, abandoned my leaky waders, started my car, waved goodbye to my friend. Drove away from Wyoming and that dirty, boring, thankless job, that beautiful, powerful, opposite-of-pretend job—away from those fields, those yellow eyes.

Drove away thinking about the real, the elemental.

Drove away thinking yeah, an irrigator, welcome to the club.

# Pooh Bear in Yellowstone

Once, walking a beach in San Francisco, I found myself surrounded by old men wearing only T-shirts. By accident—shouldn't they have signs or something, yellow caution tape?—I'd entered the nudist zone. In every direction, disconcertingly tan nether regions freely absorbed the golden warmth.

"Poohbearing," my girlfriend said when I described the scene to her that evening. "That's what it's called."

Poohbearing? As in sweet innocent honey-loving Winnie?

"He had just that red top, no pants. You never noticed?"

Entirely unbidden, this memory flashed fleshily in my mind a few years later, on a February morning in the Yellowstone backcountry. The sky a perfection of blue, the temperature 10 degrees at best, I was standing barefoot in sparkling powder, making final adjustments to a fat backpack prior to committing its awkward weight to my shoulders.

Skis cinched tight—*check*.

Boots secured—*check*.

To my right, a close buddy, Turner, dealt with his own gear. To my left, a cow moose, her gaze steady, seemed to ask with big quiet eyes: Are you idiots for real? The Snake River flowed smooth and strong before us, a hundred feet wide, no telling how deep. We were, of course, outfitted from the waist up with layers of Capilene and Gore-Tex—and buck-ass naked from the waist down, Poohbearing hardcore.

Why would two young fellows drop trou, drop thermal undies, drop skivvies, and subject their manhood to the frigid rush of winter water? Why would they torture them-selves so? Simple answer: no bridge, yearnings for the other side, bravery in the face of imminent shrinkage, fun.

Our plan was to relax, to spend four or five days touring forested valleys, letting secret hot springs determine the route. Each night we would camp beside a pool, soak for hours, sway to the soundscape of bugling swans and howl-ing wolves, catch glimpses of starlight through rents in ris-ing steam. It would be surreal, a mix of the harshest season and the cushiest luxury. To reach that luxury, though...

Maybe the moose had a point.

I hoisted my pack, gripped my poles, and stepped into the current, Turner following hot on my heels, or cold on my cheeks, as it were. Ankle-deep became knee-deep, knee-deep became thigh-deep, thigh-deep became you-know-what-deep. Toes went numb, went beyond numb, went beyond beyond. Bones splintered, shattered, exploded in the imagination.

And then, arriving at the far bank, a tall drift of white that given the circumstances suggested a snuggly terrycloth towel, it was over, whew. The silly bear (me) and the drawer-less ursine adventurer (Turner) had done it, had managed to keep clothing dry *and* pass through the liquid gate that bars entry to the kingdom of inhuman wilds. Calves and thighs a horrifying shade of violet, we clambered out, The End.

Uh, yeah, not exactly.

The thing about fording a river at the start of a trip is that, in most scenarios, you've got to ford it again on the return. We did. After blue moonglow and elk hooves sloshing in eddies and magnitudinous solitude and hot cocoa—after breakfasts of Fig Newtons and many untracked miles and faint rosy alpenglow and the complete mesmerization that is a trillion flakes dancing into boiling tubs—we found ourselves back at the Snake. Inside a sideways blizzard. Shivering. Dreading the inevitable.

No time to waste, Turner bared himself to the whirling weather and I did the same, thinking that certain orifices aren't meant to be involved in skiing. Ready? Ready. We plunged into focus.

What focus! I swear on the cuteness of Piglet and Roo, on the sorrow of Eeyore, that the purity of our attention bore a distinct resemblance to spiritual awakening, to enlightenment. The universe contracted to the now-now-now of inching progress. The do-or-die intensity led consciousness toward a rare and marvelous clarity.

Water, snow.

White chaos, burning pain.

Though the entire Yellowstone outing was fantastic, a waking dream of elemental reality, this crossing is what I recall most vividly, what I cherish above all else. This Poohbearing. This Poohbearing in winter. This crazy agonizing gleeful Poohbearing in winter. This getting from here to there.

~    ~    ~

# UTAH

# The Unknown Country

Deanna Glover's voice hits a high note along with her eyebrows, tone and expression conveying the same grandmotherly concern. She's not *my* grandmother—we met for the first time an hour ago—but that hardly seems to matter to the sweet, white-haired eighty-year-old. "Tell me you'll have a friend hiking with you, because it's a lot of country," she says, gripping her walker. "And, you know, I start to worry."

The Kanab Heritage Museum, in Kane County, Utah, is cluttered with arrowheads, wedding gowns, antique farm implements, and sepia photographs of the families that founded the town in 1870. I phoned Deanna, a descendant of these Mormon pioneers, earlier this April morning, and though the museum, her baby and brainchild, was closed, she insisted on opening it so that the displays could inform my upcoming two-hundred-mile, two-week trek through Grand Staircase–Escalante National Monument.

Hiking with a friend? I shake my head, and a latent anxiety rears up, the prickly fear-thrill of engaging a desert that demands resourcefulness (drinking water found in sculpted potholes), extreme caution (camouflaged rattlesnakes in the middle of the trail), and a tolerance for solitude (my girlfriend, as I hugged her goodbye before leaving for Utah, told me to enjoy peeking into the recesses of my own skull).

Recounting this quip about the intracranial vista to Deanna, I notice her grip on the walker tighten. "Oh, I'll be praying for you, then," she says. "I'm not kidding—it's a whole lot of country."

~

Ocher buttes, umber scarps, maroon hoodoos: whole lot of country indeed. Extending north and east from Kanab, Grand Staircase–Escalante National Monument encompasses one of the gnarliest stretches of the lower forty-eight. Geology, that's the word. Borrowing author Charles Bowden's apt phrase, "the heart of stone."

Ever since President Clinton established the monument in 1996, it's been contentious: old-timers versus newcomers, Republicans versus Democrats, advocates of *using* the land versus advocates of *conserving* the land (as if these were mutually exclusive agendas). Conservative politicians in pressed blue jeans and blazers tend to see the monument as an assault on economic growth. Dirtbag adventurers in Chaco sandals deem it the epicenter of North American slot canyoneering. In Kanab, mention Edward Abbey, the Southwest's iconic nature writer, and you'll receive a high five or a tirade, depending on your interlocutor.

The latest dispute began on December 4, 2017, when President Trump cut the 1.9-million-acre monument into three units, reducing the overall area by almost 50 percent. As outlined in the official proclamation, the White House's stance was that the Clinton administration had designated more terrain than the law allowed. Deposits of

coal, oil, and natural gas obviously played no part whatsoever in the decision—*obviously*. Environmental orga-
nizations immediately filed lawsuits, arguing that Trump
lacked the authority to shrink an existing monument.
Nevertheless, the Bureau of Land Management went
ahead and drafted plans that, if implemented, would open
approximately seven hundred thousand acres to mining
and drilling. With the final decision tied up in court, nobody can predict whether the original boundaries will or
will not be reinstated.

My interest in the place is personal. Working for the Forest Service in my twenties, I resided in a cabin an hour south
of the monument: bought my groceries in Kanab, thrashed
myself silly every weekend (for fun) in the intricate backcountry of arroyos and yuccas and coyotes. It was upsetting
to picture the wilderness ransacked for profit, to sense my
cherished memories of the region disappearing into the ab-
straction we call "news."

Thankfully, I didn't forget Almon Harris Thompson.

Nicknamed Prof, Thompson was a school superinten-
dent–cum-cartographer from New England who wore a
bushy mustache, abstained from smoking tobacco, and, according to a colleague, was "always 'level headed' and never
went off on a tangent doing wild and unwarranted things."
John Wesley Powell, the Civil War veteran famed for boat-
ing the Grand Canyon's whitewater in 1869, was Prof's
brother-in-law and boss. Together they were employed
by the federal government, a congressional appropriation
funding their brave, meticulous research into the geography of the Colorado Plateau's remote canyonlands.

"Remote" is an understatement: An 1868 military map of

Utah delineated a Connecticut-sized blank space. In 1872, at the age of thirty-two, Prof led a small party into this "unknown country." The last river to be discovered in the continental United States (the Escalante) wet his dry throat that spring, and the last range to be named (the Henry Mountains) registered his horse's hoofprint.

Emotions rarely inflect the spare prose in Prof's diary, a document devoted to mileages, elevations, the shapes of watersheds, the dips of strata, cold rain, and "a sort of dysentery attack." What does come through, however, is a seriously badass route that, by chance, flirts with our modern monument's boundaries, weaving in and out of both the Clinton and Trump versions.

For the next two weeks, I'll attempt to retrace Prof's route (he took twenty-five days), mostly by walking, occasionally by hitching. The itinerary that earns Deanna's worry and prayer has me heading northeast from Kanab: up Johnson Canyon, past the Paria amphitheater to the Blues badlands, along the headwaters of the Escalante River, through the Waterpocket Fold, and over the eleven-thousand-plus-foot Henry Mountains. In my pack I'll carry a sleeping bag and headlamp, two single-liter water bottles and a four-liter reserve dromedary, and not much food other than instant coffee, pita bread, and salami. Hopefully, beer and potato chips will greet me at the few-and-far-between gas stations—in Cannonville (pop. 175), Escalante (pop. 802), and Boulder (pop. 240). I'll lug no tent, no toilet paper, no GPS, no smartphone.

The goal is to drop below politics—to find, and to hear, the lovers who love this unique landscape. Even better, the goal is to drop below conversation, below language, and viscerally, with my own ache and my own thirst, contact the ground itself.

~

April 10 is my departure date, until it's not.

The visit with Deanna runs long, so I decide to spend the afternoon riding shotgun beside forty-three-year-old Charley Bulletts, the soft-spoken, quick-to-laugh cultural-resource director of the Kaibab Band of Paiutes.

A local boy, Charley left for a spell—tried his luck in Cedar City, Utah, and Mesquite, Nevada—but now he's home, raising his kids in this desert that raised him. His grandfather, one of the last medicine men of the tribe, was born nearby. If the Kanab Heritage Museum situates the monument within a frontier context, Charley's perspective, which he shares as we drive the outskirts of town, links it to an even deeper oral history.

"This is so bad it's comical," he says early in our tour, parking with the windshield framing a cartoony mural on a supermarket's cinder-block wall. The painting depicts a procession: covered wagons, livestock, dogs, young men carrying rifles. "I get a kick out of it, I really do—the happy Mormons entering an 'unpopulated territory,' following their destiny."

Southern Paiutes have inhabited this region since "time immemorial," and their songs make reference to woolly mammoths and flowing lava, among other bygone creatures and forces. For generations the rhythm of human life was, by necessity, synchronized with the rhythm of seasons: *When the rabbitbrush turns yellow, the pinyon pine's nuts are ready for harvesting.* The modern concept of private property, unsurprisingly, didn't exist. "Fences did it," Charley says. "After they sprang up, and we crossed them, and we got shot at numerous times, then we understood that land could be owned."

Focusing on the mural, almost like he's addressing it rather than me, Charley elaborates on this difference in worldview. "With European culture, it's pieces of paper that tell who you are and where you come from—your birth certificate, your deed. But for my people, tradition instructs us that once your baby's umbilical cord comes off, you have to put it under either a young tree or an ant pile. That way your kid can be connected to a place."

He shifts the truck into gear, and momentarily we're part of the wall's cartoony procession. Then we're cruising, our talk gaining momentum: tortoises, earthquakes, prejudice, fisheries, alcohol, dams.

I ask about the monument, figuring the subject can't be avoided, and Charley answers with grim humor. "If we let this man, this businessman, run the country, the end of the world might come earlier than we want." The joke isn't funny—isn't supposed to be funny—and neither of us smiles. On the whole, we spend far less time talking current events than talking "old ones."

After discussing the Native American Graves Protection and Repatriation Act and pausing at a site where a reburial ceremony was held, we pull into a gravel lot overlooking a reservoir. Charley's grandfather used to tell of certain spots along the road where he'd seen spirits, where you wouldn't want to change a flat tire alone in the dark. This is one such spot: The remains of fifty-three bodies were unearthed here during construction.

It doesn't look like much, metaphysically speaking.

Swallows fly with their reflections. Pebbles line the shore. Kanab's buildings stand toylike in the distance, backdropped by angular red ledges. But this nondescript quality, I suspect, is the very point: *Everything* isn't visible to *everybody.* I try to envision the scene in spring of 1872—a timber stockade and a scattering of adobe houses, Prof sorting supplies, tinkering with his theodolite, glancing up, seeing a problem to solve, a mapmaker's challenge.

Charley nods at the horizon. "People always say, 'Oh, it's desolate!' But no, that's not desolation. Spirits live out there. Beings live out there."

Out there. It's where I'm aimed. Tomorrow.

⁓

Strolling the paved road in Johnson Canyon the next morning—the road wending through the Vermillion Cliffs and White Cliffs, low steps in the gigantic topographical staircase for which the monument is partially named—I catch a glimpse of Trump's scissor work. Like most of the snipped parcels, this zone east of the road appears unaffected: no drill rigs, no ATVs tearing cryptobiotic soil crust to hell, no indication that the tilted slabs and twisty junipers have undergone a transformation. Says a sudden voice in my already-getting-dehydrated brain, *A cut on paper draws no immediate blood from the earth.*

Thirteen withering, solitary miles later, I top the Whites, turn onto Skutumpah Road, and slump down in a heap, the 85-degree heat having extracted its toll. Pure serendipity: A dented pickup with a cooler strapped to the flatbed eases to a stop alongside me. Forgoing the usual "hello," the driver mentions that people like him might not get a lot of ranching done, but they sure are good at leaning against the truck with a cold beverage at sunset. It's the long day's second voice—Quinn Robinson's voice. I hobble over on blistered feet for a Gatorade dripping with ice slush.

"Suppose I've been anywhere you can see," Quinn says, gazing across a rolling sagebrush bench bordered to the north by the Paunsaugunt Plateau's limestone ramparts (the rim of Bryce Canyon National Park) and to the south by endless violet sky. "With our few hundred acres private and the permits, well, I couldn't say how much land it adds up to." He rubs his brow, as if to massage loose an exact number. "Put it this way: five hours on a horse east from the ranch house, two hours south—we summer our 250 head on all that."

The ranch house—renovated by his dad atop the foundation initially laid by his great-granddad—is about two miles off, in a hollow, spitting distance from the monument's western margin. Quinn was homeschooled there, but he skipped grades seven and eight because "you learn more working." Cactus Ropes ballcap, oversized belt buckle: He's twenty-three years old and has twenty-two years of cowboying to his name, give or take twelve months.

Between tilts of Gatorade, Quinn calmly articulates the frustrations of keeping the family ranch going: ramping prices, scarcity of available grazing allotments in the monument, the need for a couple sidelines (he's got a degree in welding). Great-granddad Malcolm ran a herd of a thousand cattle on the Skutumpah Terrace in the early 1900s, but that type of open-range operation is out of reach in the twenty-first century.

Regardless, the dream of an uncomplicated time persists. The Robinsons, Quinn tells me, prefer to manage their home landscape for "productivity," without government agencies butting in and "locking things up." They favored the monument's reduction, hoping it would put more acres in play. "But it didn't help us anyway," Quinn says, "because the cuts weren't around here."

That's it for politics. The sun is now sinking behind a scrim of clouds, patches of ground—fifty feet away, twenty miles away—pulsing with a blush light. For a while, nothing moves but that light, including our conversation. We're mesmerized, entranced.

"Love's kind of corny, but I do love it." Quinn gives the cooler a friendly pat. "And it's not only the land. You get on a horse and ride the same places your dad rode when he was your age, and his dad rode, and his dad rode. You call them by names passed down the generations, names that aren't on any map. You do the same chores, maybe think the same thoughts. Shoot, it goes back and back."

Gatorades finished, he tips his ballcap's brim, straps the cooler tight, hops in the truck, and suggests a campsite, a snug cove edging Thompson Creek. Black exhaust uncoils from the tailpipe. I'm alone. Sort of.

*Thompson* Creek? I'd forgotten about Prof. Sure enough, there's his name on my map, labeling a blue thread that enters the monument just beyond the Robinsons' ranch house. And there, too, is the day's third voice, speaking up to me from one of the diary pages I photocopied at the Kanab library: "Friday, May 31. Broke camp at 8:00. Traveled 16 miles by 3:00, when we came to a beautiful valley with a fine cool spring in it, and we camped.... Country over which we have passed rather rough."

~

According to a friend of mine from Boulder, a speck-like village in the heart of the heart of stone, the roads in southern
Utah follow pioneer trails, the pioneer trails follow Native
American footpaths, the Native American footpaths follow
bighorn sheep tracks, and the bighorn sheep tracks follow
faults, breaks, creases—any available weakness. It's an elegant schema, an image of travelers stacking through time.
Whether you're Prof in 1872 or Wannabe Prof in 2018, stub-
born bedrock is in charge, pushing this way and prodding
that way, providing scant options for forward progress.

I leave Thompson Creek at eight a.m. on April 12, eager
to knock off a significant portion of Skutumpah Road. A
mere seventeen seconds into the march, though, an employee of WinGate Wilderness Therapy, an outdoor treatment facility for troubled teens, offers me a ride, and despite
the pep in my step, I accept. Jouncing along, my chauffeur,
Teague Perkins, mentions that "there are sixty kids in the
monument as we speak, sitting with their thoughts, some
of them detoxing." She also mentions a "magical" denizen
of the canyons, a luminescent deer-man hybrid named the
Guardian who monitors the backcountry.

Fifteen minutes later Teague drops me at a trailhead so
that I can make a detour into the narrows of Lick Wash, a
gorgeously cross-bedded feeder of the Paria River. By the
time I return to Skutumpah, the morning's warmth has
been replaced by a chill. During the next seven hours of
walking, it gets colder. And colder.

That night—*whoa*! No, I don't mean an encounter with
the Guardian. I mean forty-mile-an-hour gusts and a snow
squall: hunkering, shivering, cursing myself for under-
packing. Tossing and turning beneath a spastic tarp, I wait

for the darkness to give so that I can yank my sneakers on and go.

The upside to creeping hypothermia is that it cracks the whip. I make fifteen miles by noon of day three, descending into the Paria amphitheater, a shattered, rainbowed, kaleidoscopic basin, at the bottom of which sits the hamlet of Cannonville. Christa Sadler, whom I've arranged to meet at the town's BLM visitor center, is ahead of schedule, and she passes me in her pickup. Window rolling down: "It—is—blowing!" Blond hair tangling with dangly turquoise earrings: "Get—in—here!"

A science teacher and environmentalist based out of Flagstaff, Arizona, fifty-six-year-old Christa swung a paleontologist's rock hammer in the monument before it was designated as such. Specifically, she swung that hammer in the Blues, a two-thousand-foot-high barricade of fractal badlands adjacent to Scenic Byway 12, east of Cannonville. We camp there, sharing the misery of another bitter night, and rise early on April 14 for an excursion into the unknown country of prehistory.

Christa requires no caffeine to jump-start the day, her manic energy firing nonstop. "Fucker," she shouts, right hand forming a fist around a rolled map that highlights Trump's cuts. We're sorting supplies on the truck's tailgate, loading snacks and sunscreen into her daypack. "Where is the monument? Are we even in the monument anymore? Honest, I've never cursed so much as in the last eighteen months." She musters a fresh batch of curses for emphasis.

Our plan is to reconnoiter the Blues, the core of which remains protected, the northwestern corner of which has been excised. The Kaiparowits Formation represents, arguably, the planet's best record of terrestrial late-Cretaceous ecosystems, while the Straight Cliffs Formation below it represents, to some, a profit in the offing. Christa has published a book about the monument's superlative paleontological resources (more than a dozen dinosaur species identified over the past couple decades), and she knows plenty about the coastal swamps that deposited copious organic matter (i.e., future coal) in the Straight Cliffs. Hence her breathless venting as we strike off for six hours of scraping in the Kaiparowits dirt.

Inhale. "I've rafted the Grand Canyon about ninety times, educating other rivergoers and whatnot, but this place is extra special to me because there's still so much to discover."

Exhale. "I don't have kids. This place is where my love goes. This place."

Inhale. "What's happening to the monument has been worse than any of my breakups, ever. Problem is, instead of wanting to kill myself, with this I want to kill someone else."

Exhale. "Okay, let's set the crap aside for a bit and prospect. I could use some prospecting."

Prospecting is the search for fossils, plain and simple. Our outing, which yields hundreds of petrified-wood shards, a bunch of clamshells, and three bits of dimpled brown turtle carapace, demonstrates to me that it's a distinct mode of ambulation as well, a quirky style of being. To prospect, abandon the trail. Blur your eyes. Meditate on the delicately patterned, crumble-at-the-slightest-touch ground. Meander and scan. Scan and meander. Stay loose, open to whatever emerges.

"It's called float," Christa says. "That's our name for the stuff eroding out of these slopes and floating to the surface, indicating there might be something worth digging for nearby."

"The float zone," I say.

"The float zone," she echoes. "You've got to get in that headspace."

This coinage inspires her to share an anecdote about prospecting the Blues in the 1980s, era of Walkman and cassette tape. Alone, classical music crescendoing in the headphones, she wandered away from the so-called real world and temporarily lost herself in the *realer* world of textured earth and potential. That the anecdote doesn't mention a jaw-dropping find—say, a new-to-science dino skull—strikes me as significant. The point is just being in and with the land.

Memory transports Christa, and when she returns, the morning's cursing, the outrage and sorrow, are absent. "I can never come out here too often," she says. "Never."

But where, I'm soon wondering, is out here? Consulting the map, I can't tell if we've veered from the protected section of the Blues into the BLM's open-for-business district. It all appears of a piece. For now.

～

Christa invites me to join her and some fellow paleontologists for dinner that evening in Escalante, nineteen miles east of the Blues. I hem and haw—I'd not expected so many rides—but the offer is interesting, hard to pass up. Notwithstanding Prof's disciplined leadership, my trip takes a turn toward the random, and I spend two days in town. On Sunday, exiting Escalante, I chat with an octogenarian his-

torian who suffered a stroke and struggles with the Prof anecdotes he recounted confidently in his prime. He and his
wife, the gentlest of couples, longtime critics of the monument, insist that I spend the night in their guest bedroom.

Finally, on Monday, I again roam the backcountry
alone—Antone Flats, Death Hollow, nameless slickrock
alcoves. After seventeen miles I'm back on Scenic Byway
12, pounding pavement. An ache develops in my hip, disappears, reappears. The ache doubles down. The ache swaps
hips. I dawdle—feast on the remaining salami, sleep eleven
hours, spend the bulk of an afternoon journaling—before
limping onward.

Day ten, lips chapped to splitting, nostrils scoured
bloody by relentless blowing grit, I crash at my friend's
home in Boulder, the speck-like village surrounded by in-
cised tributary canyons of the Escalante River that, according to Prof, "no animal without wings could cross." Wait a
second. Do I have wings? How did I get here? And is this
whiskey in my mug? I've slipped into a state of dopey de-
tachment. Increasingly, I'm losing the sequence, the order:
Tropic Shale, woman who feared I was lost, scampering lizard, Canaan Peak, potsherd.

"You'll flip for Grant," my friend says, pouring another
dram.

I drain it. The hip tingles.

"Really, Grant has the Escalante's nooks and crannies in
him like nobody. Wait until you see his house."

⌁

Grant Johnson has been exploring the Escalante canyons
since 1975, and for twenty-two of those years, while running
a horsepacking guide service, he spent five months annually

in "the wild spaces." Working sporadically during his winters off, the chip-toothed, barrel-chested sixty-two-year-old dynamited an orange bulb of Navajo sandstone to create a network: den with bookshelf of obscure geology tomes, jam room with PA system and harmonicas, larder brimming with foods harvested from his Deer Creek homestead. Totaling 5,700 square feet, the dwelling is nothing like a dwarf's dank hovel and everything like *Architectural Digest* melded with *The Flintstones*.

It's April 21, day eleven. I snagged a ride here from Boulder with my friend, the two of us peering into a frenzy of snowflakes. Prof didn't swing this far south—he kept to the Aquarius Plateau, a forested behemoth hidden by the morning's swirling gray weather—but given the conditions, ascending said behemoth is less than appealing. No part of me regrets deviating from the historic route, perhaps because I'm a wimp, perhaps because I bedded down on the deck last night and woke soggy. To understate the case, I'm psyched to be a guest of Grant's sheltering caves.

"There's only one suspect crack in the whole structure," he says, craning his neck, inspecting the nearly invisible fracture with a squinting focus. We're perched on stools at the kitchen counter, a bazillion pounds of sand swirling in ancient compressed stillness above our heads. "But heck, my life will be over before the thing collapses."

That life is eclectic, an obsessive passion for the unknown country's hideaways (obscure pictograph panels, secret springs) lending coherence to what might otherwise appear a random mishmash. Grant landed in the region as a teenager, taking quarters off from college in Washington State to apprentice with itinerant uranium miners. He cofounded the Southern Utah Wilderness Alliance in 1983; for his activism he was hung in effigy by the antienviro faction in Escalante. He stabilized Ancestral Puebloan ruins alongside professional archeologists and hauled supplies for AmeriCorps crews eradicating the invasive Russian olive. He built roads and fought the building of roads.

"Everywhere that I hadn't been was my goal," Grant says, passing a bowl of steaming black beans enriched with salsa from the previous summer's garden and bacon from the former pet pig. "But there's too much for anyone to know it all." He passes a spoon. "More you know, bigger it gets."

I'm enjoying the restful lunch, but my host is antsy, the sunshine burning off this morning's overcast reminding him of neglected chores. "I better get my ass busy and milk the cow," he says, not getting his ass busy. Unfolding my map prompts him to unfold a map. Shortly, the counter is papered with hogbacks and rincons, features labeled Lamp Stand and Wolverine Bench, and we're nerding out on the minutiae of Prof's journey.

"I haven't used a topo in ages," Grant says, explaining that, fundamentally, it's the mystery of the wilderness he's after—the *beauty* of the mystery. I ask how he squared his role as a guide with the task of introducing clients to the Escalante's unguidable essence, and he says that sometimes, though he had the group's whereabouts dialed, he'd linger atop a gargantuan prow, stone-faced, incommunicado. "My clients would freak. 'What's going on? Are we in trouble? Do we know how to find camp?' I'd let that moment hang. Even if it lasted, like, thirty seconds, they had to deal."

He slides his index finger across the overlapping maps:

east from Deer Creek on the Burr Trail Road, out of the monument, through the warp of the Waterpocket Fold (centerpiece of Capitol Reef National Park), up to the crest of the Henry Mountains. The finger pauses there, as if catching its breath.

"Dude, I seriously do need to get my ass busy and milk," he says. "Aw, but can you imagine? Can you *imagine* this in 1872?"

"I've been trying," I reply.

"Me too. Since I was a teenager." He lifts the finger. "It's pretty much all I've done."

~

Days. They pass. And I pass through them, trading the monument for Dixie National Forest, the forest for Capitol Reef National Park, and the park for Notom-Bullfrog Road, which parallels the eastern flank of the Waterpocket Fold. On the fourteenth day out from Kanab, instant coffee flooding my bloodstream and the Henry Mountains looming, I'm hit with a dual realization. One, the trip is concluding, Prof soon to spin a 360, absorb the panoramic view, ink his understanding onto the American atlas's remaining white space. Two, this conclusion must for me be mute, inarticulate, the time arrived to shun characters, perspectives, varieties of dedication and fascination and love.

Grant was the last local whose story I heard, more than forty-eight hours ago. My hip is throbbing again and the temperature is climbing into the eighties again, but none of this really matters because I've got twenty-seven nonnegotiable miles to make, uphill. I've been planning this grueling ending since the beginning: trudge a knobby BLM road, bushwhack the scraggly forested slopes above Pennellen

Pass, gain the alpine ridge of Mount Ellen's south summit (named for Prof's wife).

Sneakers laced tight, I hike the complex mess spilling from the Henry foothills for five, six, seven hours—squiggly passages with vertical walls, scorched mesa tops, mauve and dun and apricot soils. Prof's diary consistently downplays challenge and travail ("Could not find trail so went up canon exploring side canon. Find trail out. Have not found one yet"), but an assistant's report mentions that at this point on the route, the party pickaxed notches into the rimrocks and wedged their shoulders against the equines' rumps to heft them over these impediments. Referring to southern Utah's contorted topography as a maze is lazy and clichéd. That doesn't alter that fact that it is a maze.

Painfully, by inches, the dark mass of Mount Ellen nears, resolving into detail: conifers, talus chutes, wizened snowbanks. I apply myself to the task of making those details *more* detailed and, simultaneously, the task of quieting my brain with exhaustion. For some reason though, in spite of the heaving effort, my brain won't quit. At treeline, the range's crest an hour distant, the symbolic finish approaching, I'm still occupied by words.

The words, it turns out, are my own.

People think they have the monument pegged, what it's made of and, accordingly, what it should be made into: a coal mine, a cow's supper, a preserve for scientific investigations, a stirring wilderness experience, an anchor for family history, a political token, a sacred grave to receive our prayers. But if enough people know something, and if they know that something differently, is that something actually known? What I've learned from two weeks of walking and hitching—two weeks of listening, both to people with my ears and to the ground itself with my ache and my thirst—is that there are layers upon layers to this famously stratified land. Always more layers. Untold layers. And that to interpret the place via a single layer is to miss the place, to know nothing whatsoever of its truth.

So goes my little monologue, a distraction from ragged lungs and cramping quadriceps. At dusk I achieve the desired spot—the mental spot (blank mind) and the physical spot (pad of crunchy grass straddling the mountain's narrow spine). I'm dazed, depleted, barely able to spread my sleeping bag, entirely *unable* to wrap my belief around the scale and power of the scene. The new monument sprawls within the sprawling old monument. Both monuments sprawl to the horizon and beyond. Limitless naked desert, as I remember it from my twenties, as I hope to always remember it, is here beneath me and before me: strange, spooky, utterly unknowable, utterly unknown.

I can feel Prof close, scribbling in his diary, disagreeing: "Sunday, June 23rd. Fred sketched our trail since leaving Kanab. Got it done at 5:00 P.M., when we started on our way back." Not wanting to interrupt yet unable to withhold comment, I speak to him, whether aloud or just internally it's difficult to say. *You tried your best, buddy, but you failed. You had to fail. Look at this. Look at this. Mapmaker, there was no possibility of succeeding.*

And then, at last, the words really are gone, swallowed by silence. The view is saturated with black, the black sparking with stars.

～  ～  ～

# ARIZONA

# The Drop

Mike and I are sitting at the edge of an anonymous prow that juts from the Grand Canyon's North Rim, seventy miles past the nearest town. It's not a large campsite, maybe ten feet square, but it's flat enough to lay pads and sleeping bags across, with a dizzying plunge on three sides.

We've come here to do nothing, at least nothing that resembles anything. The plan is to nurse a bottle of beer until the sun goes down, then nurse a second until the moon rises—to enjoy the evening's swells and lulls and silky transitions. You don't do the Grand Canyon at sunset: *It* does *you*. You stare. You blink. You breathe. You grow energized and inspired, then small and humble, then empty as the river of space flowing beneath your dangling feet, against the sheer clean cliffs. So much for any plan that claims otherwise.

Two white-throated swifts arc and loop on sharp wings, flying in close, circling us, disappearing beyond the rim. A lone cloud sponges up the day's last color. All is quiet without being silent, still without being static. Mike pops his beer and I reach for a chunk of rock weathered from the surface of the prow. Mike takes a sip. In my hand the rock is heavy and warm.

*Ah, I could sit this way for eons.*

Or could I? The rock is pocked, fist-sized, limestone. Two hundred seventy million years ago, corals and shellfish lived and died in a warm, shallow sea, their bodies sinking and piling up to become new floor. Now, that ancient ground is in my hand, and call me crazy or an animist or whatever you like, but it's speaking—not magically, but concretely, as one might expect a rock to speak. A voice tingles through my fingers, pours through my wrist, races through my elbow, my shoulder, my chest and neck and mind. I extend my arm out over the abyss, listening, obeying the command as I imagine countless humans have before.

*Drop*, the rock chants. *Drop-drop-drop-drop-drop.*

The swifts swing into view again with a whine, wings almost brushing my face, and my arm retracts, the rock's voice lost. Watching the birds carve elaborate designs upon the sky, I feel as though I have taken flight, as though attention alone—pure, basic, staring, blinking, breathing attention—has dissolved the boundary between inner and outer, observer and observed. I want to grab Mike and shake him and share the good news: the universal human fantasy, to fly like a bird, it's possible! But I can't seem to turn away or conjure language or make a gesture. For long seconds, or perhaps minutes, I wheel and swerve and sit and stare, all together and at once.

When the swifts dive from sight a thick calm settles in, and the rock in my hand pipes back up. Mike shoots me a blank, dopey look—it's clear he's also been flying—and I extend my arm.

"Focus," I say. "Become this rock." Mike's legs are crossed, hands cradling the beer in his lap. "Put yourself inside of here. Tie yourself to it." He inhales deeply and I do the same, both of us gazing at the rock, at the immeasurable space surrounding it, at the place where the two meet.

Sun presses the earth, a shining golden puddle forming in a trough on the western horizon. Overhead, the sky's lone cloud stretches and separates to reveal the night's first stars. I let go—rather, something *lets me go*—and the great absence humankind has come to cherish as a symbol of beauty, wildness, and mystery rushes to fill my hand. My fingers cup a cobble of humming air, the air as light and cool as the rock was heavy and warm.

Red, russet, red, gray, rust, mauve, black: The strata blur and blend. I'm plummeting, whizzing by a cave of nesting condors, a boulder perched on a ledge, a crumbling prehistoric granary, a blooming prickly pear, a bumblebee buoyant in flight. Toward and through it all, into the canyon's stifling inner chambers, its ageless heat and solitude, I fall. *Whump.* The damp sand. Dark walls framing faint constellations. A massive noise washing my ears.

"How'd that feel?"

Mike nods, raising his beer.

The river runs brown with sediment.

# Grandma's Deep Winter Kaibab Adventure

On our way to the Kaibab Plateau we stopped at the Desert Rat so Mike could buy a synthetic top to replace the Banana Republic waffle-print shirts I'd forbidden him to bring into the backcountry. Normally I leave my friends to dress themselves, but Mike had never been winter camping or cross-country skiing and didn't grasp how speedily a sweaty cotton garment can morph into an icy straitjacket. "But I look so damn good in those shirts," he said as we entered the store, aware that the comment would freak me out.

The joint was empty save for the manager, Bo Beck, a middle-aged guy with a buzzed head who'd been adventuring in the Southwest for decades and was the author of a guidebook to local trails. Bingo. Mike went about his shopping and I outlined our plan to Mr. Beck: We'd ski the length of the Kaibab, drop into the Grand Canyon on foot for a four-day hike, then retrace our steps and ski back out. Two weeks, wilderness immersion. The cold white and the hot red all in a single tremendous trip.

Beck was the jittery sort, not really one for making eye contact, so I knew something was up when he turned and locked onto me for a beat. "Years ago I got caught on the

Kaibab in a blizzard," he said. "Temperature dropped to twenty below. Drifts rose to my bellybutton." His eyes twitched at the ceiling. "It got dark and I broke into a Park Service shack and shivered till dawn."

The story rhymed with others I'd heard: mountain lions emboldened by hunger, claustrophobia-inducing white-outs, twenty feet of snow in a season. Feeling my anxiety rising, and not liking the feeling, I excused myself to find Mike. He was on the other side of the store, a plain black shirt in either hand. "I think the Small is going to be too tight, but I'm concerned that the Medium will be loose in the sleeves," he said. "And correct me if I'm wrong, because I don't know jack about any of this, but it strikes me that baggy sleeves could really cramp our style, by which I mean the glory of the expedition."

Mike. He's a wiry blueberry farmer from New Jersey, a man of refined pleasures, most notably hot tubs, sleeping past noon, fruit smoothies, and sharing with me the nagging fear that at any moment his knees will "explode" (basketball injury, lingering paranoia). By a certain line of reasoning, he's the World's Most Unlikely Hardcore Winter Trekker, but that line fails to recognize his greatest attribute: game-ness. Mike is always game, always down for whatever, especially when he's got no clue what "whatever" might entail.

"I guess I'm leaning toward the Small," he said. "What do you think?"

The image of Mr. Beck mired in heavy powder, bellybutton-deep, flashed in my mind.

"Yeah, best to play it safe," I replied. "Those baggy sleeves have trouble written all over them."

~

A few words about the Kaibab. It's an island. No, strike that—it's a boat, a forested barge seventy miles long and thirty miles wide floating atop northern Arizona's vast desert ocean, the Grand Canyon plunging from its southern edge like some undersea abyss. Nine thousand feet high. Rugged and remote. Millions of tourists tag the South Rim each year, but only a fraction of them cross the Kaibab on its sole paved road to dead-end at the North Rim's Grand Lodge for beers and fat views.

Of course, the beers are a seasonal phenomenon. From November through May, the rim is all but abandoned, the road unplowed. Maintenance workers buzz around on snowmobiles, fixing generators and shoveling roofs, but they're a skeleton crew, and they're it. Come winter, even the mule deer head to lower ground.

In terms of history, Teddy Roosevelt loved hunting on the Kaibab, and in 1906 he designated it a national game preserve. (In 1919, when Grand Canyon National Park was formed, the preserve was split between the National Park Service and the US Forest Service.) The ecologist-cum-ethicist Aldo Leopold also spent time on the Kaibab. As did the cowboy novelist Zane Gray. As did the monkeywrenching novelist Edward Abbey. As did Everett Ruess, the West's most famous missing person, a vagabond printmaker who roamed the Four Corners region as a teenager prior to mysteriously disappearing in 1934.

And then—please, no drumroll necessary—there's Mike and me. For four summers we shared a one-room cabin on the Kaibab, rattlesnakes and bobcats our neighbors. We were biological wildlife technicians, professional bushwhackers tasked with searching ponderosa pine stands, aspen groves, and spruce-fir thickets for streaks of chalky poop and the hawks that pooped them. It was a dreamy gig, the type of job where you get so deep in the land that the land gets in you. Perfect, except for the heat.

"We should really visit in February," Mike said one particularly blistering August afternoon during our fourth and final summer of poop-searching. He was snagged by a thorny shrub, all scratched up and dehydrated and desperate for a smoothie. "Bring some sled dogs, a team of eight or so Siberian huskies? Build snowmen at the rim and kick them into oblivion?" I wasn't sure if I could handle a team of dogs, but I liked the snowman idea.

Thus was born our fantasy of exploring the plateau during the frigid *brrrrr* of its hardest season.

⸺

"I thought skiing was all about 'shredding gnarly pow' and other dumb-sounding stuff," Mike said, his voice a rent in the forest's silky quiet. He was crumpled in the snow, his sixty-pound pack (primarily tuna fish, cheddar cheese blocks, and instant coffee) having toppled him for the third time in as many hours. "Whatever we're doing *is not skiing.*"

It was our first day on the crusty white road and already we were knackered. That said, we were also buzzing, or at least I was, each pull of crisp, fresh, piney air lighting me up with a crisp, fresh, piney exuberance. We were doing it! We were back! And best of all, the weather was fine: sunny, blue skies, 45 degrees. It appeared as though Bo Beck was a bit of a mythmaker, the polar ferocity I'd been dreading a bit of a myth.

I planted my poles and sidestepped over, extending a hand. "Not so fast," Mike said. "This has just become an official rest break—a *long* rest break. And while I'm on the subject, from now on call me Grandma. But don't go picturing some sweet little lady, molasses cookies, that kind of bull." He spit into the snow for grandmotherly emphasis. "No sir. I'm slow, I'm bitter, and I'm positive that if we keep this up one of my knees is going to explode."

I asked which knee.

He smiled. "Both."

After lounging for a half-hour, guzzling gorp and screeching greetings at the occasional acrobatic raven, we got to it, me in the lead, Grandma—ever agonized—lagging behind. Our path went through mature forest and zones where wildfires had blackened the trees. It went through memories too, old dusty memories of those old dusty summers we'd spent schwacking the plateau. Porcupine quills, fossils, lichen, lupine, fawns gamboling, a hummingbird's iridescent throat, a mouse's bleached bones knit into auburn duff—the images rose before me, linking one to another. But they didn't belong: wrong season, wrong mood. Like the miles, they slipped away beneath my skis.

Wilderness therapy? Something like that. A week without people, without money, without internet or cars or clutter. A week for the mind's usual chirps, mutterings, and sirens to lose themselves in exertion.

That first evening looked, sounded, and tasted the same as the five that followed. Pitch the tent in pink sunset glow. Gather a pile of branches. Make a ripping fire. These were the best times, these spacey, lazy hours, hands and feet and faces too hot, backs frozen. Dinners were delicious: beans and rice from a sooty aluminum pot, melted smoky snow-water, cheap whiskey straight out of the plastic bottle.

I'd take a nip and mention my steaming socks. Grandma would take a nip and describe his plans for establishing a smoothie company in Philadelphia ("maybe Manhattan if it does well"). Coyotes yowled in the distance. Flecks of ash drifted mothlike and mute above the flames. In the darkness the huge land became snug, a cozy chamber roofed with stars.

As anticipated, the huge land soon became huge again, very huge. It's one thing to experience the Grand Canyon, another thing to experience it in winter, a third thing—a thing best expressed by a sequence of joyous, meticulously arranged swear words—to gulp consecutive pots of Taster's Choice while perched all dangle-legged and agog out front of the shuttered, half-buried Grand Lodge. For two days we toured the desolate rim, sharing the world's most famous vistas with a friendly squirrel and an electrician named Jude (pale, wispy) who may or may not have been a ghost. We climbed rock outcrops. We peed off the edge. We built a mini-snowman but didn't have the heart to kick him.

A part of me would have liked to stay there, gazing and tossing snowballs into the abyss, but another part felt tugged by gravity: The depths were calling. So on the ninth morning of sun, having imbibed enough caffeine to permanently damage our brains, we stashed the skis beneath a ledge and started down. "The time has come to regain our sacred pedestrian heritage," Grandma proclaimed, triumphant.

The descent was a shedding of layers, both clothing and rock strata—the Coconino Sandstone and our jackets, then the Hermit Shale and our gloves, then the Supai Group and our hats. Icicles dripped. Junipers sloughed snow. By the time we hit the Redwall Limestone, winter was gone, melted and forgotten, and I was hiking in my boxers.

Fourteen miles to the river. A night in the dirt. Black-throated sparrows. Fragrant sagebrush. Another ten miles to a twisty tributary canyon where a creek flickered through bare gray cottonwoods. We camped there, at the foot of soaring cliffs, at the hot hidden middle of immensity, and steeped ourselves in a stillness stiller than any I'd ever encountered. It was a geologic stillness, primordial and dense. Shouting, singing, clacking stones together—these somehow added to its power. It was all-encompassing, all-swallowing. Clouds scudded in. They were gorgeous. They were part of it. We thought nothing of them, nothing of anything, and the afternoon passed in reverie.

But the reverie refused to hold. Stillness? What's this *stillness* of which you speak? The next morning, roused by the tent's crazy flapping, I stuck my head out into whirling chaos: snowflakes swooping and swerving over cactus and yucca, rusty red towers vanishing and materializing and vanishing again. There was no sky, just storm, just frenzy. Winter was back, pressing in from every side. Apparently the Kaibab's sneaky white hand had reached low during the night to grab us from our sanctuary. And now that we were grabbed, it was squeezing.

"Rough out there, though beautiful too," I said, wiggling into the tent and zipping the door closed. Grandma emitted a high-pitched whining noise and burrowed into his sleeping bag, only emerging for a quadruple-dose of instant Taster's. We drank without speaking, the tent sucking and snapping against our ears. I thought of Bo Beck's story, thought of his mired bellybutton, and my anxiety surged. If the storm was this bad *inside* the canyon, what was going on *atop* the plateau, six thousand feet higher?

The tent shuddered, jerked, heaved like a punctured lung. Our trail back to the rim was twenty miles, narrow as a sidewalk, carved into vertical walls—a daunting prospect even in stable weather.

"I'm paranoid about my knees," Grandma said. That was all.

⌣

An accomplished travel writer once told me the problem with building suspense in a first-person adventure story is that the reader knows, from the outset, the narrator is going to make it out alive. He put it quite logically: "If the author croaked in the wilderness, then who the hell is sitting at the computer typing it all up?"

This by way of saying that—surprise, surprise—we didn't croak. Grandma made it to New Jersey and indulged in the most decadent jumbo smoothie of his life. I treated myself to a post-trip trip to Palm Springs, California, where I lounged poolside with real grandmas (the nice molasses cookie kind).

Nevertheless, things did get weird, get bad, get miserable to the point of scary. The storm unloaded its screaming Arctic-style violence onto us for a full seventy-two straight hours. Ice froze in our beards and to our eyebrows. Curses mixed with prayers and confusion. The climb out of the canyon nearly killed us, the next day *did* kill us, and the day after that we rose to Heaven, where, incredibly enough, we were killed again.

Whew—it was over.

But obviously it wasn't over.

~

Day fourteen. An open meadow at the geographic center of the plateau, a wondrous place all glittery under sun. Not that I had energy left for wonder. The blizzard was spent, but the road—a direct shot to our car, still forty miles north—was buried by three feet of powder. As in gone. As in oh-mercy-my-measly-muscles-can't-press-on-like-this-oh-mercy.

We'd been trudging since five a.m. and Grandma was coming apart, falling farther and farther behind. I paused to check his progress but couldn't make him out—the snow was too bright, the distance between us too great. Fearing that this time his knees really had exploded, I sat on my pack to wait. A plane cut a line through the blue at thirty-five thousand feet. I tried to picture myself up there, tried to picture the tray tables and peanuts and sodas, the speed and ease of it all. Nope. That reality wasn't real to me.

I was cold.

I began to shiver.

I was where I was: *here*.

When Grandma arrived he didn't speak, only grimaced. "We're going to be okay," I said, offering him half of our last granola bar. "If I keep breaking trail at the rate of a mile an hour, and if you keep limping, and if we ration our food ever so slightly, I swear, we'll be out of here in four days, maybe even three, I swear."

Silence. Grandma pondered the fragment of granola in the palm of his mitten, scrutinized it with a strange and disturbing intensity of focus, and after a horribly prolonged minute, raised it to his mouth. As he did so, two crumbs fell to the snow. They were just crumbs—puny, insignificant, hardly worth a calorie combined—yet they were also more than crumbs. I saw us in them: so tiny, so trapped, so deep. You might say it was a spiritual revelation, a sudden glimpse of eternal truth, a burst of holy perspective. You might say it was the simultaneous high and low point of the entire trip, the gift we'd traveled so long and hard to receive. You might say it was the essence of the Kaibab—our special summery Kaibab transmogrified by winter.

I felt shaky.

The crumbs seemed almost to pulse against the blinding white.

And then, in the corner of my eye, I noticed another crumb, a dark crumb-speck on the horizon. Grandma let out a whoop and threw his hat in the air, took off his skis and threw them nearly as high. Impossible, a hallucination: metal and fire and power, the strength of a thousand horses, the determination of ten thousand men. The crumb-speck was our salvation, our freedom—a beast of a John Deere tractor ramming through the drifts, blasting them out of existence.

We stared the idiot-stare of exhaustion and disbelief, the plow blasting and blasting and blasting until it stopped beside us. The driver opened the door. He was wearing a brown Park Service collared shirt, sleeves rolled up, no jacket or expedition gear. His hair was combed, his mustache trimmed. This gentleman looked like he was en route to the supermarket, perhaps heading to pick his kids up from soccer practice.

"We've got to get a couple of trucks to the rim this afternoon," he said over the noise of the engine. "If you boys are tired of skiing, I've got the road cleared all the way out. Should be easy walking on the whole."

It didn't make sense, nor did it matter. The driver nodded and the snow burst skyward. Grandma danced a jig.

"Let's burn the skis!" he hollered. "Let's burn them and stroll ourselves out of here in style!" His boots clicked on the road's hard surface. His arms and legs spasmed with an energy I hadn't seen in days. "To Las Vegas! To all-you-can-eat buffets! To quitting cross-country skiing! To the rest of our lives!"

The plow was soon a mile away, a crumb-speck again, the land both bigger and smaller around it. Though I firmly opposed burning any of our gear, I didn't want to let Grandma down. I clipped out of my skis and joined the celebration. That conversation could wait.

# Old Friend

Do you remember the time? I was driving, you were sitting to my right, the summer day was blurring by—aspen, Doug fir, northern flicker, Steller's jay. Neither of us knew what the heck we were looking at, some moving thing the color of the road's dirt and, in places, in the pattern of leaves, the color of shadow. The windows were down, the radio off, the jeep bumping along. I eased us to a stop and the animal stopped, twenty feet ahead. We cursed for joy. We sang dirty words of surprise and disbelief and gratitude for our good fortune.

I'd never met a bobcat in the wild, never looked into a bobcat's face and felt a bobcat looking back, and neither had you. It really shut us up, that feeling, really paused our mouths and minds. It sounds cheesy, but it's true—the eyes, those eyes. We stared and the bobcat stared and the shared staring bonded us, everything deepening and stilling. Catching a glimpse of a secretive animal is one thing, but catching a secretive animal catching *you*, appreciating the mirrored fascination, seeing that it has a face like yours, with ears and nose, a mouth and eyes, and that it casts its senses into the world like a soft net, as you do, as I do, and with that net retrieves the faces swimming out from the shadows and the sun...

What can I say? It shut us up and shut us up fast. That seems to say it all.

But do you remember the thing that happened later, after the bobcat broke the trance, disappeared into the woods, after we drove away, talked, swore some more, laughed and felt blessed and went quiet? What I remember is sadness. No, what I remember is *shame*. My outward gaze turned inward. I realized we'd done wrong.

That bobcat we saw, that bobcat we admired, what did it see? Bumping along again through the shadows and sun, the blur of aspen and Doug fir and woodpeckers and jays, it hit me in a painful way—a jeep. Bobcat gave its perfect body and we gave a jeep. Bobcat gave its eyes and we gave a windshield. In return for fur, we offered steel. That bobcat we saw presented itself honestly, but we did not. We took without giving. We absorbed without being absorbed. Unaware that we were doing so, we played ourselves off as a machine.

Sure, it would be easy to say that the bobcat didn't care, only stopped in fear or shock, that bobcats don't cast their senses like a soft net into the world as we do, or for the same reasons. But you were there. You saw the eyes. It was trying to look. It was looking. I can't say what exactly it was looking *for*, but I can say with certainty that *it was looking*.

Beers. A dip in the pond. A bonfire that night, the flames licking up, the owls hooting and scooping overhead. We told the story and our friends were excited and since then I've told the story to others who also were excited. But now I'm telling a different story, the story I felt when the jeep bumped along and we both finally went silent—the story of imbalance, of seeing but not being seen.

Old friend, it's been years since we were last together and I know this is late in coming and I know you're busy and all the rest. Please, though, I have a request. From time to time, step out into the world as yourself—not your car, not your house, not your clothes and socks and hat and sunglasses, not your shampoo and soap, not your blaring music, not your little screens, not your machines. Quit stealing yourself from the soft-flung nets that would snag you, the eyes and ears and noses and mouths that would see and hear and smell and taste you. Offer yourself to the millions of lives that knew you and me and everyone in the recent past.

I'm not saying the critters of this earth will thank us. I'm not saying they will care. I'm just saying that we can take a few breaths and step out. And that if you do this, old friend, I will do this. And that I'll look for you there.

# Long-Distance Relationship

I call Sophia and she asks what's new. We haven't spoken in a week. I'm cold and tired and don't feel like talking. The wind is blowing, the pines loud overhead. I pull my hood up, tell her what I can of Arizona.

For the last three nights running a great horned owl has perched on the same branch in the ponderosa snag across the road from the pond. Last night, he took a bat. It was dark but the sky still held a bit of blue, just enough to contrast with the bat's black wings and the owl's black legs. The legs shot forward, retracted. It happened maybe four feet beyond the tip of my nose.

The aspens a mile down the road on the right are beginning to bud, though the aspens on the left, a mile farther, haven't started. I've been jogging to the second group each afternoon, checking in. Wednesday was cloudy. By the time I reached the first group—rain. By the time I reached the second group—snow. It snowed hard, then stopped. Then more rain.

Today I counted fifty-six dark-eyed juncos, twenty-two mule deer, and four wild turkeys. I counted northern flickers but lost count. A locust thorn stuck my pinky finger near the third joint, close to the nail, and the pain, though quick, was distinct. I found a red-breasted nuthatch's cavity-nest. I also found some porcupine quills, two coyote scats, and what I'd like to think is a badger's sett, but really I have no clue.

A silver balloon, the shiny kind sold at supermarkets, got caught in a sapling. I released the balloon and it floated up, stalled, softly dropped. Written across the balloon with an orange marker were the words "Happy Birthday Mom, Love Hugo."

Oh, yeah, somebody hit a rattlesnake. It was dead on the road. I thought the dead snake was a stick. I ran the stick over with my truck.

The conversation swings to California, to Sophia, to her stories of fogbanks, mockingbirds, people in wheelchairs, people shrieking, cute dogs, a few long city walks. She went searching for the red-shouldered hawks we saw in the eucalyptus grove at the edge of the park last year—no luck. Leaning against a tree, she can smell the ocean as we speak. Parrots chatter in the tree's crown. She lifts the phone and I listen, but the parrots don't sound like much. More than anything, they sound like static.

A cloud crosses the sun. A folk singer's name is Tangled Oak. A cormorant died on the beach. Its eyes opened wide, opened wider, and closed. Three grains of sand were stuck to the left eyeball. Sophia witnessed the final breath.

After half an hour, we stop talking. I can hear sirens on her end of the line and she can hear wind rushing the pines on mine. Neither of us wants to hang up, so we don't. Our foreign worlds meet in the space between words, as if there were no Great Basin, as if my forest and her metropolis, her California and my Arizona, as if these were pressed one against the other, tight as two bodies. It's unnatural, a false geography, like maps ripped apart and collaged together, and it leaves us feeling bad.

I'll call again on Saturday. Same time. Love you. Bye.

Sophia cuts to silence and a single snowflake slants past my face. Don't ask me how I know, but I do know, for certain, that this is the last snowflake of the year. Winter is gone, spring sliding, summer approaching. The birds are nesting and the aspens are budding. It will be months of small stories separating this snowflake from the next.

If you feed a relationship these stories, can it grow? Can it live on such passing wonders?

I stand still, totally still, as though moving even slightly will break something important, something I do not understand. Almost dark now, the early stars are barely showing. I'm thinking the great horned owl will appear, that it would be a fine time for him to declare his presence.

Nothing comes. Cold, tired, phone in pocket, I walk away.

It's tough not to call Sophia back and tell her about that snowflake, that last snowflake of the year, that diagonal line in front of my face. And it's tough later, when I so badly want to tell her about the owl, the owl not seen but heard, out there, somewhere, hooting in the distance.

# Doug

The Douglas fir was 150 feet tall, perhaps taller. It leaned over the meadow, a steep green propped against open sky. Once the day's work was through, once the great horned owl's round vowel had filled everything and faded to silence and filled everything again, I liked to tamp tobacco into my pipe and have a leisurely smoke. Rest my head against the cabin's parched clapboards. Stare at the tree and forget that I was staring.

This was Arizona, the Kaibab National Forest, those years when I ascended ropes and lifted from bulky nests of sticks the not-yet-fledged hawks that my boss, an ornithologist, needed to see up close. I'd settle the birds in a bag and lower to the ground. I'd wait for measurements to be taken, blood to be drawn. I'd flinch, an angry mother stooping, screaming. Then I'd haul, set the birds in place, check my knots, and rappel.

The canopy was new to me, a secret home above my home, and I couldn't get enough. So it was hardly surprising to hear, following two cups of strong coffee one aimless Saturday morning, the Douglas fir calling my name. I wiggled into a harness, dressed in loops of webbing and clanking carabiners, crossed the meadow. Solo. Uncertain. The best way to make friends with a giant tree.

There are methods that allow for a safe rise through boughs, tricks to gain the heights, but these technical details are unimportant. What's important is the hour of *higher-higher-higher*, the meticulous gripping and pulling, how such tactile intimacy, such focus, becomes a kind of portal. To which magical realm does the portal offer passage? To this realm, nowhere else. To the secret home of shiny black ants and gymnast squirrels and baby birds. To the mazy body, the labyrinth of bark and space that houses hundreds upon hundreds.

The Douglas fir, *Pseudotsuga menziesii*, is monoecious, meaning individuals bear both male and female cones. Still, he was a he. After that first exploration, that long afternoon of breezy sway and drifting pollen clouds and butterflies in the belly, my evenings smoking outside the cabin were different, altered. *Old man, how you been? Anything to report?* Doug didn't answer, of course, yet somehow he always answered.

Four seasons in the field, summer plus summer plus summer, countless fine Saturdays aloft. My sister visited from deciduous Vermont, land of maples, and I guided her through corridors of needles, chambers of resinous air. We strung hammocks just below Doug's top and lounged until sunset, talking about Jonah and the Whale, about greater beings swallowing lesser beings, about ants, squirrels, spiders, bats, the many lives that live their lives inside larger lives.

Alas, by standing fast as young men chase their futures, elderly trees come and go. The raptor study ended and I said goodbye to Doug, got involved with coast redwoods, aspen groves, other jobs and other things. Now, a decade out, my mind returns to those countless fine Saturdays aloft. Opening the paper, clicking the laptop's news, it's too damn easy to feel as though what's holding your life is a complicated wrong, that you reside amid horror, that the hug of your habitat, your home, this world, is all toxic waters and flaming skies and gape-mouthed children stabbing fingers at their dusty bellies. And drone strikes committed in your name. And blatant thievery. And loss.

Oh, but across the meadow and above the meadow, through the portal that *is* the Doug and leads *into* the Doug, oh, another truth emerges. The truth of an alternative scale. The truth of a timeless hug. I go there often in memory.

Purple dusk. Owl's round voice filling the entirety of Arizona. My buddy Zak, from the research crew, is straddling a branch, switching on his headlamp, and I am rappelling, leaving him in the leaning crown. Later, free of gear, resting my head against the cabin, I puff my pipe and watch Zak's floating glow, a tiny dot of light within Doug's dark hugeness. That's the glow of a man who is an ant, a squirrel, I think. That's the glow of a man who, like me, like everyone, is a baby hawk.

Honestly, I never much enjoyed bagging those babies, never much enjoyed stealing from bulky nests and lowering to the dangerous ground where we humans go about our dangerous business. Giving them back to their secret home, though, setting them there gently, carefully, looking around for a moment, breathing deep before checking my knots— that was really special. Even after I'd hit the duff and unroped, even after I'd walked away, a piece of me lingered in the canopy. I suspect that piece won't ever come down. Or maybe I hope.

# Big Canyon

The canyon is big. For the sake of this story, let's call it Big Canyon. Let's call it Arizona. Let's call it August, a heat-blasted weekend, no plans.

My boss—crusty government biologist with a passion for prehistory and a back-of-the-hand backcountry knowledge—gets to reminiscing over black morning joe. I jot zero notes, pretending I can commit his verbal map to memory.

Eleven of us. Five cabins and three picnic tables. A remote field station in the woods above the desert.

Saturdays like this—for adventure.

~

*Hey, you lazy sleepy sonofa...*

Mike is groggy but game. Always game. A proper buddy.

And we're off. Twenty miles by jeep, the warren of sandy tracks increasingly confused, the pinyons and junipers sparse, then sparser, then gone. We park the rig. Take a piss at the rim. Take it all in.

*How much water did you bring?*

*Some.*

*Let's do it.*

*Indeed, my broski.*

With a gallon of sunscreen on our necks and arms, floppy canvas hats on our heads, we pick our way—step after careful step—into the cracked earth.

Trails? Yeah, right. That's why we've got bossman's instructions. Follow A to B to a spot where you'll be able to glimpse C. Contour eastward. Drop through pink sandstone ledges, maybe two hundred feet, maybe three hundred. Once you've hit the bottom, turn left. Hike the wash. Scan the north wall. Pay attention.

At the house-sized boulder, well, enjoy the shade but realize you've gone too far.

～

We're lost, stumbling.

What did bossman say, something about one with red earrings, one with a long penis, one panel where gods parade among turkeys and sheep? And spirals, didn't he say something about spirals?

We're doing the heat. We're done by the heat.

Shrike with hooked beak, perching nearby. Phoebe with peachy belly, grayish nape. Three ravens, six if you count the flying shadows. In the binocular's dark tunnel I almost feel cool, refreshed.

Really, though, what did he say?

It's not scary—being here, being in and with this wilderness—but it's not easy, either. Intense. Intensity. Afternoon gold hammering the mind flat, each blow telling us to turn around, return on a cloudy day, try again in winter. Telling us Big Canyon is big and we are small, so very small.

*Yo, let's keep going, huh?*

*Definitely. I wanna find that panel.*

～

It happens slowly, quickly, outside of time, inside the guts of time. Inside geology. Inside our blistered, light-shot brains. Inside the outside, the great outdoors.

We're stumbling until we're stopping, standing, staring. We're alone until we're not alone.

A flipped switch. Awareness.

Peoples—human peoples, animal peoples, squiggly abstract peoples—everywhere.

Unblinking. Eyeless.

We gaze and gaze.

~

Hours later, Mike has turned in for the night and the stars are thick overhead. We're drinking whiskey, boots up by the bonfire, me and my crusty boss.

*So it went okay?*

*Oh, amazing. Your directions kinda sucked*—chuckle, chuckle—*but eventually we found hundreds. They were scattered, tucked into nooks and crannies. Just needed a tweak of perception to see 'em.*

*A special spot, eh?*

Hmm. A special spot, certainly. But how to answer?

What I'm thinking is ravens, their shadows, the heat, the sandy roads, the smooth stone, the ancient stone, hands spreading pigment, hands reaching up, today and tomorrow, millennia past, the wandering, the stumbling, the thirst—how there's no separating anything, no difference between the place and the experience of the place and that long penis we call art, that turkey we call image, that squiggle we call a pictograph or a god or a mystery or whatever.

Tip the bottle. Another snort.

*A special spot, a killer Saturday.*

*I thought you'd like Big Canyon.*

~   ~   ~

# COLORADO

# Creeking

I went to the creek and stumbled on a six-point buck, field dressed, hollow. The next week I crept past a man sleeping in a nest of rags below a bridge. Foxes weave trash-paths. Addicts shout from brushy hideouts. Once, a US Geological Survey employee in waders taking sediment samples spoke to me of two girls, how they drowned downstream.

By winter I was putting in eight-hour days, bashing through brambles, crawling through tunnels, falling through ice. Hobbies like playing piano and hanging with friends were slowly displaced, the creek's waters rising inside me. Come spring I was flooded: I knew what scared me and what fascinated me and what filled my head with muck. Someone called it *creeking*, and that name sounded right.

I was a college student with childhood at his back and the entire West before him—new landscapes, new prospects, new adventures, same old dream. What I found, instead of mountains rich with gold, instead of open range and cowboy freedom, was the underside of a city, a nature sunk in concrete gullies, funneled toward resonant culverts, pinched against the howling freeway and the coal plant's fuming chimneys. What I found was unexpected: the dead buck bent across a patch of damp ground. Kneeling at the water's edge where plastic bags collect, I peered into its vacant gut.

Really, I didn't question it much at first—not the buck, but the creeking. Maybe I was tired of books and words and talk. Maybe I was uncomfortable inhabiting urban sprawl. I don't know and it doesn't matter. These things just sort of happen.

Suited up in rattiest jeans and rattiest jacket, I walk uncertain neighborhoods, traverse a weedy lot, drop to my belly, squirm a chain-link fence's ragged hole. A shallow band of water cuts the bottom of a dirt slope, and I follow, hopping from tilted stone to tilted stone, rotten log to rotten log. The creek grinds deeper, banks rising, buildings rising with them, until I'm picking my way through a gurgling, shadowed corridor with sixty-foot walls. I wade. Pigeons imprint the sky. When I climb out, it's dark and I'm far from home.

Colorado Springs wasn't a single creek, I realized, but a complex network, a web of fluid paths feeding one another, winding for miles. At sunset I'd go to a bridge and watch leaves and feathers and plastic scraps boat about on the current. I'd spit and watch it glide. Those evenings, bronze light spilling from the clouds, it seemed that I too could travel, without purpose and without thought, along the place's streams.

I started carrying a daypack with supplies: headlamp for tunnels, carrots for a snack, a lighter, a water bottle, a jackknife. Rambling, observing, I mapped in my mind the spot where two raccoons climbed a cottonwood, where a crumpled tent collected rain, where a rock rolled beneath my boot and threw me to the creek. I gathered images and experiences as my jacket gathered burs, grew heavy with them as my jeans grew heavy with mud. At night I'd sit in my room and fan everything out, the pebbles from my pockets and the scenes of the day.

On and on and on—it went on like this for a couple of years. Increasingly, I understood the city as a skin of pavement and concrete stretched over the living earth. Strolling some random street, I'd hear water, track the murmur to a grate, press my ear close, wonder where it was journeying and if a guy could join. The surface became less real to me, less joyous and less sad. Increasingly, I understood myself as one of those raccoons climbing the cottonwood, a creature endlessly exploring spaces torn between civilized and wild.

But that's dramatic, that's the words running off with themselves. Honestly, nothing notable happens in the creek. A syringe stabs mud. A lady screams at a retaining wall. Foxes weave trash-paths. Foxes pause, sniff, keep going. You pursue. You notice. You see stuff down there, that's all. You see the wind in plastic bags, the bags writhing and sucking and wheeling. You see a dead buck, his flesh stolen, his fur and bones turning to sand, washing away, grain by glittery grain.

# *Relittering*

The author Ed Abbey was famous, or perhaps infamous, for tossing empty beer cans out the window of his pickup. Hell, he'd say, it's the damn *road* that we should be calling litter. This style of provocation dates back to the Cynics, a gang of Greek ethicists who came on the scene after Socrates died in 399 BCE. They were interested in drawing attention to *nomoi*, cultural conventions that go mostly unnoticed and, accordingly, mostly unquestioned. For guys like Antisthenes, Crates, and Diogenes, acting outrageous in public was a favorite pastime.

Despite my wholehearted agreement with Abbey's point about the damn road being a damn road, there's a part of me that thinks his behavior was, well, sort of dumb. Adding trash to an already trashed planet is patently unnecessary, not to mention crude. Furthermore, this can-out-the-window radicalism has itself become a cultural convention, a standardized symbol of defiance. If the goal is to shake things up, another Budweiser in the ditch isn't going to do the trick. Maybe we need a new outrageous act?

Personally, I'm a fan of *relittering*.

The story begins during my years as a philosophy student in Colorado Springs. Once or twice a week (more if I was reading a miserable text like Hegel's *Phenomenology of Spirit*) I'd leave the dorm an hour before sundown, black Hefty bag in hand. Something about collecting the city's refuse—Styrofoam cups and cigarette butts, broken bottles and cigarette butts, rags and wrappers and crumpled papers and cigarette butts—freed my mind of words, concepts, big theories. It will sound paradoxical, but filthy trash consistently swept my headspace clean.

Unsurprisingly, the initial dozen outings ended with me at campus, struggling to lift my bulging bag over the rim of a dumpster, fearful of catching a corner and leaking *Eau de C. Spgs.* onto my noggin. That is to say, I prettified the cityscape by consolidating strewn garbage and transferring it to a socially sanctioned receptacle. A no-brainer: Where else would a good young environmentalist offload thirty thick gallons of disgusting junk?

Alas, philosophy teaches us little more than how to confuse our settled opinions. Soon enough, I was wondering why a giant metal box brimming with rubbish was not a blight, and from there it was just a hop and a skip to the local dump, where, one hot Saturday morning, I watched bulldozers busy themselves with heaps of stinking, steaming waste. Their work reminded me of a neurotic friend who "cleaned" his room by tidying clutter into some seventeen neat piles.

*All we're doing,* I realized, *is pushing this awful shit in circles. If it ain't recyclable, it ain't recyclable. Period.* I understood, instantly, that pure intentions and elbow grease wouldn't green up a single inch of a society that overproduces and overconsumes. It hit me as gut-level sadness: *This is your home. Welcome.*

Relittering was thereby invented.

It felt mighty awkward at first, so I started small. At the edge of a park or playground I'd stoop, pluck a wadded napkin, then walk five blocks and gently set it beside a bus stop. Within a few months, the napkins had become pizza boxes, ratty jackets, tires yanked from overgrown lots, shredded blue tarps excavated from the creek's compacted sand. The artist in me wanted to consciously arrange, to fashion a thing of beauty, but my inner Cynic wouldn't allow sugarcoating. He insisted that this was about forcing a raw confrontation between the citizens of Athens (C. Spgs.) and their milieu.

The task was relocation, plain and direct. Haul nastiness from abandoned spaces—the undersides of freeway overpasses, the insides of concrete drainage tunnels—and set it in the sun, preferably in a spot where it wouldn't cause extra labor for a municipal janitor or landscaper.

These days I live in a rural area, and while there's definitely plenty of garbage around, it appears manageable against the backdrop of undeveloped nature, which means I typically shoo it into a trash bin. I miss relittering, though, I really do. There was an absurdity to it, a black humor that helped me laugh in the face of our drive toward ruination. It was a grimy, tactile encounter with the truth of culture and place—what Henry David Thoreau would have called "Contact! Contact!"

Funny that old Henry should butt in here, as he, like Ed Abbey, was also an heir to the Cynics. Different eras call for different techniques, I suppose. One fellow finishes his Budweiser and rolls down the window. A second kicks that can out of the ditch, into plain view. A third borrows an ax, heads to a pond on the outskirts of town, and builds himself a cabin, a dwelling apart from—a dwelling that stands as a rebuke of—his mad, reckless age.

And then there's Diogenes. He wore tattered clothes, resided in a wooden tub on the street corner, ticked off both Plato *and* Alexander the Great, and allegedly said, "Humans have complicated every simple gift of the gods." If such a generalization causes discomfort, tough noogies. That's the idea.

# When We Curse Peaks

My buddy Chris and I were famous back in college, at least to ourselves, for our many and varied defeats above treeline. To put it nicely, our vision and verve outstripped our technical climbing ability. To put it less nicely, we were incompetent. Once, attempting a notoriously exposed ridge in December, Chris forgot both pants and boots; he had his ice axe and crampons, but just bald sneakers for the feet and thermal underwear for the legs. Another time—okay, twice—we failed to even reach our desired trailhead, let alone the base of the route we had planned to ascend in "perfect style." It demanded some effort, to be sure, but when it came to *not* bagging Colorado's high peaks, we were the absolute best.

Regardless of whether we did or didn't ink our names in a summit register, much fun was had on these outings. There was the bivouacking in remote cirques, the alpenglow's soft fade, the cheap whiskey, the singalongs, the enlivening wind, the slurping of cold beef stew from a tin can when somebody—who could that be?—spaced the stove. Shaggy white mountain goats, lovely as clouds, would pause to look at us with their deep eyes. "Take me to the top," I'd say, making sure Chris overheard. "This guy in the thermal undies means *nothing* to me. You are the most beautiful beings on the planet. *Please*, take me with you."

Of course, there was also vigorous, impassioned cursing, for a misadventure without swears is far less enjoyable than one loaded with scatological references and creative anatomy lessons. When our subheroic assault on some fourteen-thousand-foot granite hulk was stymied by pissing rain, poor rope management, a misread map, or a hangover from the aforementioned whiskey—well, let's say that our mouths glowed neon with blue language, like we'd swallowed our headlamps or something. Think of John Muir's elegant syntax, those ornate sentences lavishing praise upon the divine order of nature, only dirtier.

To be frank about the depth and breadth of our degeneracy, the dirtiness often started before we found ourselves stuck on a sketchy, chossy, dead-end ledge or playing hide-and-seek with lightning. Driving from campus to the mountains on Friday afternoons, a kind of manic energy crackled in the car, the sight of intimidating ranges out the window inspiring us to disparagement. Chris especially had a knack for belittling the horizon, for building himself up by putting the earth down with taunts, challenges, and macho nonsense. By no means was it genuine hubris; we knew our wings were made of wax. It was play, that's all, what the basketballers call trash talk. Still, I cringe to consider how ugly and offensive it would have sounded to an outside observer.

That's where this gets interesting: outside observer. In my reading of contemporary eco-literature and my spotty study of indigenous North American spiritual traditions, I find again and again the marvelous, mysterious, brain-bending notion that the so-called inanimate world—the world of "objects" without human ears—is in fact listening to what we two-leggeds say. The hunter must take care not to offend the deer and bear, but he should hold his tongue in the presence of plants, stones, rivers, weather systems, and stars too. We all should. It's a matter of manners, of simple respect.

So, then, was our repeated defeat in the alpine zone due to irreverent chitchat and outright blaspheming of the sacred topography, or did it stem exclusively from sloppy mountaineering? Perhaps more important, were we being disrespectful in the first place, or did the land know it was just a joke, just friendly ribbing? It certainly never *felt* like we were behaving rudely.

Another pal of mine, easily the funniest guy around, has said to me many times, usually after cutting into some soft spot of my ego with a simultaneously incisive and hilarious remark, that humor is the greatest form of honesty. I'm inclined to agree, and to add that honesty is one of the core fibers in the muscle we call the heart. Without honesty there can be no true love; there can only be a kind of rose-scented fake love, Hallmarky and shallow—a love that resembles some endless honeymoon, not a real marriage, warts, F-bombs, deprecating jokes and all.

I picture my girlfriend, how her eyes shine with glee as she mirrors my idiocy back to me, exaggerating it, hugging me with it. I picture my sister, my mom and dad, all my closest companions, how what bonds us is the willingness to laugh at one another's expense, and how that laugher itself becomes the external marker of our connection, our appreciation, our camaraderie.

These days Chris is climbing glaciers in the Pacific Northwest, earning his keep as some kind of businessman, living a life that does not involve me. I mostly hike on my own, in silence, without the aid of whiskey; if I do get drunk it's on thin air, and if I do speak aloud it's probably to utter— good gentle fellow that I am—some little poem of thanks and praise to the ground beneath my boots. However, from time to time I'll take a seat way up there above the trees, in the tundra meadows or among the jagged rocks, and listen through the memories of those missions Chris and I made into the glorious, rugged, ambition-smashing Colorado backcountry—those trips we threw ourselves into with all the stupid youthful energy of energized stupid youth.

What I hear in such moments of reflection, albeit filthily expressed, is a kind of pure passion: rough and real, unedited, totally vulgar and totally true. I hear crazy yelling, cackling laughter, words unfit for print. I hear my dear old buddy leaning into the wind and sleet and danger, his voice barely audible over the louder, larger voice of storm.

Hearing this, I relax, at ease with the land. Then I stand up, stub my toe, and cuss so forcefully that the sky trembles and the boulders shake, almost like the mountain itself is chuckling.

The last laugh is always on me.

# In Praise of Scrambling

I first heard the noun "scramble"—defined by the *Oxford English Dictionary* as "a mountain walk up steep terrain involving the use of one's hands"—when I was eighteen, bumming around bonnie Scotland. *Bonnie* Scotland? More like wet, windy, tent-thrashing Scotland. My traveling buddy, a mostly inscrutable, mostly inebriated Glaswegian who cared naught for dental hygiene and knew naught of mortal fear, had initiated a rest break (smoke break) during our approach to the Black Cuillin's Pinnacle Ridge. Features with fierce names like Sgurr nan Gillean and Basteir Tooth loomed overhead—a traverse far riskier than anything I'd undertaken back home. Reared in Vermont, I was a bushwhacker accustomed to dirt and ferns, not alpine gabbro.

"Oh, come now, it's only a wee scramble," the Glaswegian said between puffs on an immense unfiltered rollie.

Scram*what*? Only a wee? Had this bloke been nipping minibottles of Glenfiddich at breakfast?

"A wee scramble," he said. "You'll be fine."

An hour later I was marooned on a crumbly ledge in twisting fog, the Glaswegian stemming up a grim, grimy chimney nearby—stemming and whistling to himself, the unflappable bastard. Reaching for a heinous little nub of a

136

hold—gulp—I simultaneously reached my personal limit. *Too stern,* an inner voice said. *You're a hiker, a hillwalker. If you want to tango with Sgurrs and Tooths, go ahead, learn ropes and anchors and whatnot. Please, though, don't be a damn fool.* Acceding to this sage advice, I retreated, slightly ashamed, majorly relieved.

But here's the thing: Nursing pints in the pub that evening, buzzed on Guinness instead of adrenaline, I couldn't stop thinking about that ledge, that chimney, that heinous nub of a hold. They were in me as question marks, as possibilities, as promises of…hmm, I wasn't sure *what* they promised. I was sure, however, of my desire—my need—to find out.

The wimpy Yankee kid was hooked, lickety-split. Hooked on scrambling. Hooked on the ancient art of walking landscapes with one's hands.

～

Picture it starting with some Cro-Magnon fellow crawling up a rock rib in search of berries. Picture Roman legionaries scaling outcrops to better view the battlefield. Picture nineteenth-century guides in knickers and hobnail boots summiting those very Scottish Highlands that puckered me. Fast-forward to the present, in which speedy unroped alpinists make short work of the casual pitches that punctuate their multiday Patagonian enchainments. Tomorrow, perhaps, we'll enter a postindustrial future—no Petzl, no Black Diamond, just primates scrambling once again for survival.

Which leads to questions. Is there an instant of transition where Class 3 hand-walking leaves off and that revered, outrageous genre of ascent—the free solo—begins? Is Alex

Honnold, modern master of the free solo, a glorified scrambler? Would he take offense at the suggestion? What of Tom
Patey, hero among Scottish hardmen, a guy who prior to
his death rappelling in 1970 unabashedly clutched grassy
tussocks when they appeared at the perfect, desperate,
knee-knocking moment? Did *he* give a hoot about labels
and systems of classification, or was his concern only the
topography and the challenge—the challenging fun—of
fitting his body to its shapes?

The rigmarole of so-called serious climbing (painful
shoes, crotch-binding harness) strikes me as contrived. At
the sport crag, over the clinking of quickdraws, you hear so
much *bomber*-this and *bomber*-that, as though the bliss of
"good rock" is all that matters. But last I checked, the ma-
jority of this planet's intriguing nooks and alluring crannies are anything but solid. Should we disregard the chossy
gullies and exfoliating gendarmes in pursuit of the cleanest,
sweetest lines, or should we accept them, celebrate them,
rejoice in their vitalizing difficulties?

Here's my response: Thank you, sir, may I have another!

And this also: Technical mountaineering, with its req-
uisite gear hoard and skill set, plus its narrow focus on, say,
a particular flared crack, has for me felt like a door closing,
whereas scrambling—unfettered, minimalistic—has felt
like a door swinging open to reveal the sprawling earth's
limitless wonder. That wonder includes mountain goats
drifting across fanning talus, moonlight reflecting from a
midnight lake whose shoreline tundra serves as a pillow, a
rain-slicked ramp fast becoming a hail-greased slide, a double rainbow culminating in the pot of gold that is a family of
blond marmots—the list goes forever.

Scrambling is too often deemed an obligatory chore to

be dealt with begrudgingly: a means to achieving more vertical, more complicated objectives. No longer. I praise scrambling as an *end in itself.* Part hiking, part jogging, part clambering, part cowering, part pulling jugs, part pulling shrubs, part dangling above the abyss, part chilling in wildflower meadows, part badass, part goofball—it amounts, in sum, to a choose-your-own-adventure story, fluid and liberating.

The typical Cro-Magnon fellow would, I suspect, enjoy spending a day in the hills with me, screwing around, romping wherever we fancy.

~

Less than a year after the Scotland trip—having investigated the Camel's Hump summit in Vermont, met with perverse fascination the Trap Dike's crux corner in New York, and gotten giddily scared all through Huntington Ravine in New Hampshire—I headed west. According to my parents, the plan was an undergraduate degree in Colorado. According to their son, it was rugged country and visceral thrills.

Enter my childhood pal Craig—his callused fingertips and stoic grit. The name derives from the Scottish Gaelic *creag*, meaning "rock," and indeed he always has been a rock-tough dude, the ideal comrade for peak-bagging road trips. Each August, the Toyota Tercel filled to brimming with beer, mac and cheese, sunscreen, granola bars, scratched mountaineering helmets, a banjo, more beer, and our ever-intensifying sweat-stench, we crisscrossed the Mosquitoes, Indian Peaks, Sangre de Cristos, and Sawatch, seeking out the higher education most overpriced colleges fail to provide.

The seeking went something like this: sleep in dirt, wake in dark, tape blistered heels by headlamp, chug instant coffee. Sending routes we would inevitably send boulders tumbling and, if only in the uncanny movie theater of imagination, send *ourselves* tumbling too. Nerves, concentration, fatigue, elation. Then the dazed descent and the delicious hoppy beverages we'd stashed in a creek's cool eddy. Then the car, the winding road. Then the next massif, its flying buttresses lit briefly with peachy alpenglow. Then five hours of anxious dreams.

But which massif, there being so many options in the skyrocketing Rockies? Integral to the selection process was *Colorado Scrambles,* authored by Dave Cooper, a transplanted Englishman (yet another nutty Brit). You wouldn't think his slim volume could pose a fatal threat to a pair of healthy youths, but by the same reasoning you wouldn't think it could give them life—give them crackling exuberant *aliveness*—which is, on numerous occasions, exactly what occurred.

Take, for example, our excursion to Capitol Peak, a notorious fourteener near Carbondale, a gray terror I'd already attempted twice: stymied by graupel squalls, stymied by a friend who doodied his drawers. With Craig's quiet confidence as the ace up my sleeve, I figured that finally it was going to happen.

It did. The dicey contour around a 13,664-foot subsummit happened. The ridge thinning into a taut granite tightrope happened. The tilted grid of ball-bearing pebbles and rotten ladder-ledges happened. A hundred yards of slinking across jumbled blocks, each looser than the last, placed us at the proper tip-top where—ah—*nothing* happened besides vast distances and hearty laughter and gnawed cheddar cheese and (shouts to the Glaswegian) an immense unfiltered rollie traded back and forth.

"You remember the deal with getting off of her," Craig said an hour later, breaking our easy reverie, cinching tight his backpack.

"Seventy percent of accidents, right?"

"Yeah, thereabouts."

With that, he inched toward the intricate messiness neither of us was eager to reengage, gripped an oddly askew, microwave-sized chunk of mountain, swung his hips wide, and for a flashing second defied the laws of gravity. At least that's how it appeared from the safety of my perch. In truth, it was the microwave plummeting, and Craig lagging behind, that made him magically hover. I watched my childhood pal palm the atmosphere, arrange himself catlike in swirling space, and—by the grace of the ineffable—land (also catlike) on the only meager shelf Capitol's plunging north slope had to offer.

Such encounters with pure physical reality stamp the scrambler, their power like a tattoo—and the ink doesn't wash off. To the contrary, it seeps in and spreads out.

The shelf was maybe eight feet down, maybe two thousand feet off the deck.

Craig looked at me, shook his head, and smiled.

～

Passion begets passion. Scrambling leads to more scrambling. Capitol becomes Pyramid, Ice Mountain, Quandary. Teewinot in the Tetons becomes Riegelhuth Minaret in the Sierra Nevada. King Lear Peak, lord of the Black Rock Desert, becomes a weeklong thicket, bears and biting midges, inspired cussing, and eventually the basaltic rubble of Vancouver Island's Golden Hinde. One day I find myself older, returned to Colorado's Elk Mountains, countless verts nipping at my heels, a thirty-foot face—ugly, mean—staring me in the face.

Progression, growth, change.

*Oh, come now, it's only a wee scramble.*

The voice is…mine?

A decade out from my Scottish initiation, the method by which I hand-walk has taken a turn for the sketchy. Purple clouds sizzling with electricity. Been there. Knife-edge ridges that are katana-sharp and threaten to split the straddler straight along his perineum. Heck, those *are* scrambling—its essence, its basic nature. No, the turn of which I speak appears, at first glance, fairly benign. Even its name— small and smooth and round-sounding in the mouth—obscures the potential danger: a shattered femur, a survival crawl, a million stars piercing the night from which there will likely be no escape.

"Solo," that's the word, the turn. Of late, I've been going solo.

What I mean is *solitudo*, the Latin mix of "loneliness" and "wilderness." What I mean is bonafide isolation, miles and miles of personal responsibility, of entrancing vigilance. What I mean is a bright-clear morning in July, three shots of espresso awakening the animal impulse to roam, to stitch earth and sky together with the thread of an idiosyncratic path.

And not only do I routinely avoid companionship, but increasingly I avoid guidebooks, trip reports, topographic maps, tips from seasoned elders, all the various forms of beta that can point a wanderer in the correct direction, give him options, mitigate his outing's hazardous unknowns. Insane, it might seem, to eyeball a jagged horizon from the valley floor, bushwhack to its base, eat a packet of M&M's, slurp a melty snowbank for hydration, and then commit, uncertain whether the next half-mile goes at Class 4, goes at 5.4, or goes to waking nightmare: stuck, sans cell phone, no detailed itinerary posted on the kitchen table because, from the outset, moment-by-moment prompts provided by geology and weather have been the sole guide, the sole plan. Probably insane, yes. Haul him off to the padded cirque!

A Sunday from last summer in the Elks exemplifies my burgeoning *solitudo* style. I'd been camping on the outskirts of Crested Butte, contemplating the monolithic red slab that forms the southwest aspect of 12,653-foot Avery Peak, hoping it would act as a kind of gateway to the convoluted network of crests and crowns farther east. Because I couldn't foretell where the uplands would spit me out and didn't want to be beholden to some pesky trailhead parking lot, I raised a thumb. Go light, as they say.

One short hitch and one aspen grove later (vicious stinging nettles), I began kicking at a snow-choked ravine, pointy red shards in both fists should, god forbid, I slip and need to self-arrest. The mother of those shards was everywhere above me, then everywhere beneath me, then everywhere inside me—burning inside quadriceps and lungs, humming inside the deepest folds of my focused mammalian brain. Melted dry and not overly polished, the slab proved an easier scramble than anticipated, and by noon I was cranking a flattish ridge. Yonder: a collage of shark-jaws and chainsaw chains that went and went and went, all intimidation and opportunity.

I paused, tied my shoes tighter, took a piss. I fidgeted, inspected my shoes to make sure they were tied, considered trying to pee again. I spun 360, spun 720, and, from that whirl of vistas, was launched.

What words to use for the next six (or was it nine?) hours of orienteering, chasing options, backtracking, doubting, questing after secret sneaks and untried passages? How to describe the pillars I hugged and the ptarmigans I flushed and the quality of pulsing isolation, the beautiful strangeness of *solitudo*? Peering at a precipice, listening for a hollow hold, gluing digits to the tiniest details, lowering myself—I grew aware of an invisible line, a safety tether that was itself nothing more than strands of awareness (*this* pressure, *this* angle, *this* balance) braided together.

Invisible line? On belay? Could it be, I wondered, what the big boys experience, the Honnolds and Pateys, the bold folks who have embraced the timeless scramble and elevated it to an art beyond belief? This attunement? This zone? This sense, fleeting and false, of being protected *from* the mountain *by* the mountain? Could this be the trusty Cro-Magnon genes scrambling, as they always have and always will, for survival?

Step.

Step again.

Hello, sun-warmed stone. Respectful nod to you, mind-trembling exposure.

At dusk, I pushed for the umpteenth time over a lofty knob, a lonely promontory. I pushed cautiously, eagerly. I pushed out of the past and into the future, foot following foot, hand following hand.

# Flying with Birds

On a bright July evening in Crested Butte, Colorado, the town's namesake landform towering three thousand feet overhead, two dudes—and "dudes" is without a doubt the correct appellation—parked their trucks between the local baseball field and a flat green meadow, which they referred to as "the LZ," or landing zone. Bo Thomsen, a plumber in flip-flops and board shorts, ate a hotdog, then smoked a cigarette. Ben Eaton, a blacksmith with a greasy foam cap and gray-flecked sideburns, turned lazy circles, inspecting distant cumulus clouds. The duo possessed a combined thirty-eight years of paragliding experience. Over the past couple of months they had flown fifty times together, most recently that very morning.

"Twice in a day is good," Bo said. "Keeps me from drinking at night."

"It only looks dangerous," Ben added. "I mean, until it gets dangerous. Then you're gripped."

Paragliding's elegance, its poet-writing-cursive-on-thin-air quality, should never be reduced to a mere equation, but here goes: body harness plus twenty-five-foot nylon "wing" plus wind rushing up a mountainside plus faith in that wind's willingness to catch you with its unseen arms equals silky-smooth bliss unknown to common, featherless mortals. Some folks set records, staying aloft for hours, traveling hundreds of miles, and others compete in nauseating aerobatic competitions. Ben learned in the Swiss Alps, where "everyone does it." Bo learned in the Rockies from a guy "who definitely should not have been teaching." They described their personal style of paragliding to me as "flying with the birds."

Gear packed and the distant cumuli deemed benign, we piled into Ben's truck and headed up Mt. Crested Butte, first on pavement, then on bumpy ski-resort maintenance roads. Bouncing along, I was told that "thermals pop off sun-warmed rocks," that "they're like invisible tornadoes," that "hawks show us where to catch them," that "it's all about finding lift," and that "you know you've reached sixteen thousand feet because the fourteen-thousand-foot peaks look like tiny bumps." I also learned that Bo's parents were hippies, that he was conceived in a teepee, and that his real name—"like, on my birth certificate"—is Bojangles. If these dudes were of the class Aves, I thought to myself, Ben would be a golden eagle, big and steady and mellow, and Bo would be a cliff swallow, slight and manic, utterly nonstop.

Half a dozen steep switchbacks and two dozen dirty Bo jokes later, we parked on an exposed ridge at eleven thousand feet, the soon-to-be-setting sun washing countless mountains—one for every compass degree, it seemed—in buttery light. An ankle-breaking talus slope plunged toward conifers that could easily snag a poorly launched pilot, beyond which the itsy-bitsy village and its bordering LZ resembled scenery stolen from a model-train set. Plastic flagging tied to metal posts indicated that the wind was "not nuking," but blowing at an easy, serviceable six or seven miles per hour.

Ben climbed into the truck's bed and tugged on Gore-Tex pants, a jacket, and leather boots. Bo lit another cigarette and commenced telling stories, the memories of bygone excitement animating his entire being, sending him into twirling, arms-wide reenactments. He reenacted crows in enormous flocks and Canada geese honking past at eye level. He reenacted red-tailed hawks playfully buffeting him and red-tailed hawks not so playfully attacking with their talons. He reenacted thunderstorms, rainbows, October's trembling aspen slopes, elk in the lowlands craning their necks, bear cubs like black microspecks, white microspecks of snow geese caressing the stratosphere.

"I think *I'm* a badass, but look where birds go," he said. "Look how they move."

Ben glanced up from strapping on a kneepad. "Biomimicry, you know?"

"Yeah, biomimicry. Fucking Batman, fucking Spiderman—the superheroes are wannabe animals. Birds are the masters, the original pilots."

For twenty minutes we discussed—we *celebrated*—the many life-forms that have evolved aerial locomotion, from soaring squirrels in New England to gliding snakes in Borneo to the millions of underappreciated insects helicoptering around porch lights near and far. "Regular people live in a 2-D world," Bo said, slowing, making his face go flat. "They think they're experiencing the mountain, biking or hiking or skiing on a trail, but that's not the mountain. The mountain is much, much more. There's swirling air, vultures coring up, energy flowing in ten directions at once."

He sprinted and swerved, stopping inches shy of the ridge's edge. "When you're flying it's totally 3-D. It's backward, forward, sideways...corkscrew higher, spiral lower...collapse the wing, aw shit...deep breath...pull through."

In his eccentric way, Bo was hitting on something thrilling and profound—that what gets called *mountain* actually swells inside the word until the seams burst and the real thing, the thing that is not a thing at all but rather a web of innumerable, unspeakable relationships, emerges in the mind. And then it bursts the mind's seams too.

Triggered perhaps by some subtle climatic cue only the initiated recognize as such, the bird men donned helmets, buckled themselves into harnesses, and prepared to launch. One moment Bo's wing was spread on the ground, limp and useless and uninspiring, a wad of factory-sewn fabrics. The next moment he was flicking the glorious invention skyward, forming it into a crescent-shaped pocket, turning, jumping, contracting his knees to his chest, slicing off through space. This transition—to intense focus, to air hissing across nylon—was startling, and it left me tingling. Ben followed after Bo, the pair of them coasting back and forth before me, impossibly distant and yet right there, graceful and close.

For a second, I stood jealous in my sneakers, the ancient dream transformed: to fly not like a bird, but like a paraglider!

Then the second vanished. It was my job, I remembered, to shuttle the dang truck down that bumpy road.

# Favor the Mountain

It's an exceedingly white January afternoon on America's sketchiest road—white flurries rushing the windshield and swirling in the mirrors, white ridges and cirques disappearing among torn white clouds. Heck, even the road is white, though it won't remain so for long. Dack Klein is behind the wheel of his eighteen-ton Mack plow truck, laughing his big laugh, navigating yet another lethal curve with all the casual confidence of a man who's done this some seven thousand times. Or maybe it's more like eight thousand times.

An equipment operator with the Colorado Department of Transportation (CDOT), Klein has worked the fifteen miles of US Highway 550 that climb from Ouray to the top of 11,018-foot Red Mountain Pass since 2003. He has worked them at dawn and midnight, on Halloween and Easter and Cinco de Mayo. He has worked them in every imaginable type of blizzard—from the fierce to the downright savage, from the protracted to the neverending—and in blizzards that transcend the imagination's paltry limits.

Forty-two years old, with a black buzz cut, a stout build, and a probably-should-have-died crash under his belt, Klein knows this stretch of pavement better than the backs of his own grease-smudged hands. Ouray's four and a half drivers—two on the day shift, one on swing, one on grave-yard, and a part-time backup for "when things fall apart"—maintain fewer miles of road than almost any of the state's other two hundred CDOT patrols. Shifts normally last eight hours but will extend to twelve or eighteen when the weather insists. Weekends are more of a theoretical possibility than an enjoyed reality, monthlong runs of consecutive days to be expected. Between late September and early June, Klein hangs with his wife and three kids way less than he hangs with his Mack—"pushing."

Milepost 90, passing below an avalanche path named Ruby Walls: "You've got to appreciate the dangers when you're pushing. Last winter we had a chunk of rock the size of a football field detach right here."

Milepost 87, entering Ironton Park, the road's only flat-tish section: "There have been nights I could barely see past the wipers when I was pushing. It can take twenty minutes to manage this one nasty mile if it's blowing."

Milepost 81, beneath the sensitive Blue Point: "The saying goes that Blue Point will run if you sneeze. Usually it's a bank slip, but occasionally it's a giant, and then you've got to do some serious pushing."

Milepost 80.28, at the summit: "Jackknifed eighteen-wheelers, four feet of fresh powder in eight hours—pushing on Red gets crazy. But that's what makes it special."

The San Juan Mountains average 349 inches of snow annually, and much of it falls twice: first from the sky, then from the crests and headwalls where it tries, and fails, to cling. Seventy named avalanche paths intersect Highway 550 in the twenty-three miles linking Ouray and Silverton, the town on the south side of the pass that serves as headquarters for another CDOT patrol. Some of the starting zones span hundreds of acres, release two hundred thousand cubic yards of snow, and generate wind speeds in excess of two hundred miles per hour. The infamous East Riverside can dump fifty feet of concrete-thick debris on the centerline and has claimed the lives of three plow drivers—in 1970, 1978, and 1992—as well as a preacher and his two daughters in 1963, and two men and most of their mule team in 1883. Since 1935, when the initial attempts to keep the road open through winter were made, dozens of people have perished trying to get from point A to point B, though an exact number is impossible to tally.

The threats are numerous and diverse: precipitous cliffs, towers of brittle ice, 8 percent grades, unexpected doglegs. Speaking with Klein over the phone before my visit, he explained that the lower portion of the road is literally chiseled into the vertical rock of the Uncompahgre Gorge—a narrow geologic throat a thousand feet deep in places—and that the upper portion, beyond Ironton Park, traverses subalpine slopes largely scoured of their trees. We talked for twenty minutes and he used the word "respect" often enough that I lost count. He also exuded a pure, childlike enthusiasm for the elemental power of the range, the clarity of purpose plowing engenders, and what he called his "Tonka Truck."

By the end of the conversation, a paradoxical invitation was on the table, repellant and enticing: *Come ride.*

So here we are at the center of Klein's world, a shiny orange 4x4 Mack, newest addition to a fleet that includes a grader, a blower, a pair of loaders, and two other plows. The holidays have passed—a three-day storm kept the Ouray patrol pushing straight through Christmas—and a fresh storm is on the rise. Our twelve-foot rubber-coated carbide blade is lowered, our ten-foot wing jutting from behind the passenger-side door on its hydraulic arms, forcing snow farther off the road. The rig costs $200,000, gets two and a half miles to the gallon, and fills the lane like a linebacker in a too-small suit. Three hundred twenty-five horses snort beneath the broad hood. The cab is richly perfumed with diesel fuel, warm and snug.

"Less spacious than your Toyota Tercel," Klein says with a grin after I mention the make and model of my car. "Little for comfort but a blast to drive."

Spacewise, the cab is indeed reminiscent of a compact—and thus concludes the list of vehicular similarities. We're seven feet off the deck, dwarfing F-350s, a sand-salt mix spraying from a massive hopper mounted to the Mack's rear. Electronics abound: ground thermometers, GPS tracking systems, so many screens and gauges I'm reminded of an airplane cockpit. A toolbox at my feet contains emergency supplies—MREs, rope, a space blanket, a Maglite, a wrench—and at my elbow Klein has wedged in an additional backpack loaded with food, water, and clothing to last two days. Avalanche beacons strapped to our chests blink, their batteries fresh.

Having tagged the top of the pass, 3,200 feet above Ouray, and pulled a U-turn, Klein and I are now descending Upper Switchbacks, a set of precarious zigzags balanced on the mountain's steep face. Pressing my nose to the window, what I notice is an absence: Despite the pathetically narrow shoulder and stomach-tightening exposure, there are no guardrails in sight. The reason, I'm told, is simple. Plow drivers don't only remove snow, they put it somewhere. On Highway 550, that somewhere is over the edge.

"We've got nicknames for everything," Klein says. "Paul's Plunge. Scary Larry's Rock. This is Upper Switchbacks, but it's also Dack's Dilemma."

The dilemma occurred in 2007 on a typical Red Mountain night: temperatures in the single digits, bad gusts, omnidirectional snow. Visibility was a few notches below poor, and a terrified kid in a sedan was hogging both lanes, approaching head-on. Given the conditions, this member of the "traveling public," as Klein affectionately terms such drivers, probably should have been at home on the couch, playing video games or making out with his girlfriend. Klein decelerated—he was doing about ten miles per hour to begin with—and eased to the side of the road.

"It was this slow-motion tilting," he says, recalling what happened next. "I kind of reached for my seatbelt, reached for the door, thinking maybe I could jump out, but there wasn't enough time." Picturing his wife asleep in their house at the base of the pass, her belly round and pregnant, he gripped the wheel and "went for the ride."

That ride dropped Klein sixty feet before the truck's cab crumpled around his body with a metallic crunch. A lower switchback had caught him, nearly killed him, and saved his life, all at once. He was inverted, half-stuck, bruised but otherwise uninjured, trying to kick through the windshield. Ten long minutes later, when a car parked and some "kind of loud, kind of funny" people got out, he was still kicking. His rescuers were absolutely hammered—aimlessly touring the storm, draining beers—but their drunken hearts were in the right place. They bashed the glass, extracted Klein, and lodged him among the empties in their back seat.

"I didn't think the roll messed with me," Klein says. "But ever since, I've had trouble getting over toward the lip in this spot."

The memory residing in his hands takes the wheel and tugs gently left, inching us away from the shoulder and the blankness—ghost white, white smoke, old lace, bone— seething beyond.

"I'm fine everywhere else, but at this spot it's like my body won't allow it. I just can't get over as far."

~

Klein and his colleagues refer to this behavior—cheating the double yellow a bit, erring on the side of caution—as "favoring the mountain." They refer to snow falling at a rate of a quarter-inch per hour or less as "nuisance snow" and to scraping compressed snow from the pavement as "peeling pack." They refer to a job well done as "safe enough for your mother" and to themselves as "a family." Neighboring patrols out of Silverton, Ridgeway, Cascade, and Norwood (the in-laws?) are the target of good-natured trash talk regarding who's "keeping it pretty" and who's "falling behind."

The Ouray shop, a seven-bay garage brimming with bull plows, rotary blades, Pewag chains, chin-high tires, and chummy bullshitting galore, perches at the south end of town where Highway 550 begins its ascent. It's a place to guzzle coffee and listen, left ear tuned to plowspeak, right ear to a possible call on the ever-crackly radio. But avid discussion of all things Red is by no means limited to the CDOT gang.

Ouray is a tiny town—eight hundred residents snug-gling on a seven-block grid that appears lifted from a snow globe—and it is made tinier by its surroundings. Brute ori-gami comes to mind, as though a trillion postcards of sub-lime scenery have been folded and refolded into an orogenic Frankenstein. The topography is unavoidable, the range young and sharp and ubiquitous, rocketing five thousand feet from the sidewalks. On slushy corners, in restaurants, at the post office, and in motel lobbies, the community's al-lotment of daily chitchat is neatly divided: 50 percent Bron-cos football, 50 percent Red.

"I was up there once in the middle of the night, return-ing from Arizona in my Mazda 626," says Robert Stoufer, who has lived in Ouray for forty years and owns Buckskin Booksellers. "A slide ran in front, then another behind. I got trapped for three hours."

The 1998 book *Living (and Dying) in Avalanche Country,* which sits beside *The Snowy Torrents* and *Colorado Ava-lanche Disasters* on the local interest shelf at Buckskin, at-tests to the 550 corridor's dynamism with countless photos and anecdotes: a mangled D-6 Caterpillar, a buried driver tunneling toward freedom with a flashlight. Many roads around the American West routinely unnerve the travel-ing public—Colorado alone boasts Lizard Head Pass (for-ty-eight avalanche paths), Berthoud Pass (twenty-five), Monarch Pass (nineteen)—but none compare to the "Mil-lion Dollar Highway." In addition to Red, this segment of 550 includes Molas Pass (fifty paths) and Coal Bank Pass (twenty), both south of Silverton. It's the most avy-prone road in the lower forty-eight.

In 1993, after the third plow driver died at East Riverside,

CDOT got extra serious about managing road-threatening slides and began a collaboration with the Colorado Avalanche Information Center (CAIC) that continues to this day. No one has been killed by an avalanche since, thanks to a mixed strategy involving teams of forecasters nerding out on the snowpack, gates that can lock the road shut when necessary, and explosives.

Take the recent Christmas blizzard. The sky collapses and keeps collapsing. A CDOT driver, eyes burning and brain aching, gets on the radio. *Hey, boss*, he says, *I think it might be time to close her.* Meanwhile two CAIC forecasters stationed in Silverton, and one stationed in Ouray, have been eyeing the Doppler radar, monitoring the slopes, cruising the road at ungodly hours, worrying themselves ragged over "what's getting loaded" and "what wants to run." More calls, more conversation, and more snow lead to a decision: *Okay, lock the gate.*

Ambulances, commercial truckers, and stoked snowboarders in need of a pow fix rely on the road being open, which means that the locked gate represents a ticking clock. Mitigation usually starts by six in the morning, weather permitting. According to CDOT's Avalanche Fact Sheet, gun crews can employ any of the following to trigger slides: "5-pound charges set by hand; a truck-mounted 'avalauncher' that uses pneumatic pressure to fire 2.2-pound rounds; a 105 Howitzer leased from the Army that can fire 40-pound missiles up to seven miles; a helicopter that drops 30- to 50-pound bombs." The debris doesn't move itself, and so pushing recommences, the clock still ticking. Klein has occasionally found himself operating the Mack, the guns, and the front-end loader all in one slog of a shift.

"Every run's different," says Elwood Gregory, who plowed the road from 1979 to 1986. A mustached seventy-seven-year-old with a bald pate, he misses "the thrill of battling Red"—those jolts of adrenaline when a baby avalanche clipped the fender or thumped the roof of his truck. "You come around a corner and there's an ermine in the road, or a ptarmigan, or a crippled elk that got swept by a slide. Or you come around and headlights are shooting out of the gorge, straight into the air. One time I saw a car burning down there, flames and everything. Turned out a guy had murdered his wife and sent her over."

What about family? What did they think about this treacherous work?

"My wife understood how much I enjoyed it, so she was fine," he says. "It bothered my mother, though. Her house was there at the bottom of the hill. At midnight I'd drive by and she would flicker the lights in her window and I'd flicker my headlights back. It was a way to say, 'You can go to sleep now, Mother. I survived another night.'"

～

Another night. It should be a bumper sticker slapped onto every CDOT truck, a tattoo inked onto every bicep.

During my afternoon ride with Klein, he emphasized that Red Mountain Pass morphs into a "different creature" with the fading of dusk's alpenglow. The guys rotate shifts— two months of days, two months of swings, two months of graves—to share the burden. However, that order fails under heavy weather, everybody pushing together to render the road safe. And even when the snow quits, there are rocks to clear, vehicles to fix, a whole series of tasks to prepare for the next dump.

"The storms usually come after dark," Klein said. "Clifford's on graves, but he's been puking with some kind of flu, so I don't think you want to seal yourself into a truck with him for eight hours. We've got to make sure you ride with Michael on swing."

Michael is Michael Harrison, a fifty-two-year-old from Chicago's South Side who moved to the San Juans after college and still retains the accent of his childhood. Compared with the ebullient Klein, he is a monk of the road, focused and intense. His blue eyes look into, through, and beyond me when I meet him outside the CDOT shop on my third evening in Ouray.

"It's fucking spooky up there," he says. "Really fucking spooky. You sure you want to do this?"

The weather that's been growing on the pass is peaking, snow falling at three inches per hour. Harrison just finished his first run, and already his efforts are close to erased. There's no time to waste: clean gunk-ice from the lights, load the hopper with sand, go. Rule number one of plowing is push *with* the storm.

Buckled into the cab, grinding uphill, it's a matter of seconds before town falls away. The temperature dives to 2 degrees in the gorge, visibility tightens to twenty-five feet, and the wind makes a menagerie's worth of animal sounds. Harrison says nothing, his right hand working the three joysticks that command the angle of the plow and wing, his left hand steady on the wheel. We're low-beaming it, squinting, billions of snowflakes flashing in our yellow and blue strobes.

*Star Wars*, I'm thinking. What by day felt like an airplane cockpit presently feels like a spaceship. Town is gone for good, a distant planet, a false memory of security and laughter and cheery neon lights in tavern windows. The edge is near, that dreaded, cosmic, one-thousand-foot drop yawning.

Milepost 90, passing Ruby Walls: "In sideways weather, I've got to be able to get out of the truck, take three steps, and touch the mountain. If I can touch the mountain, I'm safe. If I can't, that means the mountain might drop out from under my tires."

Milepost 87, entering Ironton Park: "Sometimes I catch myself saying, 'Where's the road?' I'll be humming to myself: 'Where's the road? Where's the road?'"

Milepost 81, beneath Blue Point: "This is definitely the let's-get-the-fuck-out-of-here section. You see these sloughs spilling across our lane? They came down in the last hour. That's bad. We call those indicator slides. They mean trouble."

Milepost 80.28, at the summit: "It's life and death up here, no doubt. People think you can drop a plow and go for it, but you can't. That's why so many CDOT drivers don't want anything to do with Red Mountain Pass. If you make a mistake, it will probably be your last. You've got to be on it. You've got to be in tune. You've got to be in the game, totally in the game."

Minutes later, creeping back toward Ouray, again absorbed in silent concentration, Harrison surprises me with an abrupt comment. We're approaching milepost 88, perhaps the most important landmark on the road, one I've yet to visit. "I'm going to pull over for a second," he says. "I want you to see The Monument."

We adjust safety helmets atop our wool hats, open the

doors, and exit into knee-deep powder. The storm rages, but suddenly there is no aggression to it, no threat. Inside the truck, the weather is something to fear and respect. Outside, it simply *is*—equal parts motion and stillness, chaos and calm, violence and peace.

Harrison trudges into a drift, slips a Maglite from his pocket, and illuminates a polished slab of granite that is fast on its way to being buried. Below the engraved image of a plow truck almost identical to the one idling behind us, I read three names and three dates: ROBERT MILLER (MARCH 2, 1970), TERRY KISHBAUGH (FEBRUARY 10, 1978), EDDIE IMEL (MARCH 5, 1992).

"These dudes gave their lives to keep the road open," Harrison says. "East Riverside took them all—different events but the same slide."

We stand there for a while, the names on the stone disappearing beneath delicate flakes. Soon enough the engraved plow will be resting on its own white road.

"The mountain's got a lot of different moods," Harrison says finally, without turning. "In its own sick little way, it can be kind of magical."

He switches off the Maglite, tilts his face to the sky.

"I guess we'd better get back to pushing. It's really coming down now, isn't it?"

# Dead or Alive

Fred Penasa, the proprietor of Southwest Taxidermy in Montrose, Colorado, rubs his whitening beard with a hand scarred from countless scalpel nicks and sewing needle punctures. We're standing in his showroom on a Friday afternoon, gazing into the glass pupils of a ram he shot in the San Juan Mountains. Winner of the 2006 Colorado State Taxidermy Championship in the Professional Division, this particular specimen will be descending a "rocky ridge" dusted with "snow" for the foreseeable future.

"Doing bighorns is a mixture of things—it's the animal, sure, but it's also knowing where it lived, the wilderness it called home, how hard those winters can get," Penasa says. "I'm thinking about the story, about how it all went down, and I'm trying to re-create that story for my client. Maybe it was early morning. Maybe a raven had just flown by and the ram was turning, glancing backwards."

Over the past hour Penasa has toured me around his almost two-thousand-square-foot shop and, simultaneously, the quasi-magical process by which he earns a living. Quasi-magical? How else to describe the transformation of, say, an inside-out bobcat hide—stiff and pink like stale chewing gum—to a fierce feline that seemingly might leap from its mount at any moment? Or consider the grizzly I've walked past a dozen times, each encounter shivering my spine; the bear is deader than dead, but its careful preparation expresses an intimate biological knowledge and brings startling life to the freeze-framed roar.

Penasa claims no godly powers of regeneration, no access to the Greek *pneuma* and Latin *spiritus*, ancient terms for the animating breath that literally inflates capital-B Being. In fact, he insists that decades of meticulous labor have made it difficult for him to see the animals he takes apart and reassembles as "wholes" rather than as "pieces." This isn't to imply that he fails to appreciate them—the bighorn is "majestic, plain majestic"—but that his default setting is hyperfocus, what he calls "looking and looking again."

In the early 1990s, channeling his childhood love of hunting and, more generally, staring at moose and pronghorn antelope through binoculars, Penasa left his job as a carpenter and signed up for a nine-week course at the Montana School of Taxidermy and Tanning. With all the steps from skinning and fleshing to "building your form" and "designing your habitat" under his belt, he returned to Montrose and established his business. He estimates that it's one of approximately two hundred full-time taxidermy outfits in Colorado.

"There's a high turnover rate with these backyard shops," he explains. "A lot of guys get into taxidermy thinking it's all glory, all trophy bucks, but you've got to really work hard to establish your reputation. My first five years, I was still a carpenter, doing taxidermy at night and on the weekends. I was going nonstop, trying to get things right."

While a commitment to accuracy—to realism—has long been the hallmark of topnotch wildlife artists, the profession has changed significantly since the early 1900s, both in regard to materials and techniques. To illustrate the progression from "back in the day," when the old-timers used scrap lumber and papier-mâché to make their forms, Penasa ushers me into a closet where a creepy mountain goat resides. Head lumpy, eyes pale and flat, the creature resembles nothing so much as a cheap costume in a bad monster movie. "We use foam manikins now," Penasa says. "Companies are doing synthetic antler reproductions, all sorts of fancy stuff. It's a huge industry, especially in the West."

Having locked the goat-beast into its cell, Penasa leads me to the main studio, a clean, bright, high-ceilinged space with smocks hanging from a nail in the wall and an assortment of tools—ranging from drawknives to paintbrushes—cluttering tall shelving units. It's somewhat reminiscent of an elementary school art classroom, if you disregard the shoulder-mounted ungulates in various states of finish: shiny bolts protruding in lieu of antlers, tear ducts in need of touching up.

Penasa emphasizes that despite twenty-five years of experience and five thousand North American mammals to his credit, he's still got a bunch to learn. "A big part of it is just studying the animals, knowing what they look like," he says, seating himself at a workbench. "Before Google, I was cutting photos from magazines, organizing all these scraps in folders, using them as references—how do the nostrils go?" He dumps a soggy, supple elk hide out of a white garbage bag, where it's been rehydrating in preparation for gluing and stitching. "The art is making it natural. You're trying for perfection, but you can't ever reach perfection. You can't ever be good enough."

Adjusting spectacles on the bridge of his nose, he leans over the hide, inspecting. My attention wanders away, coming to rest on a nearby mule deer, two beads of dew clinging to its whiskers; they're the tiniest details, pinpricks at best, yet they glisten, throw sparks of light.

"Mod Podge, a couple drops," Penasa says, noticing me noticing. He smiles, perhaps remembering the many hours spent molding that deer's ears from auto Bondo, its face from clay—perhaps remembering the satisfaction of applying that last dab of glue. "Brings the story in again. It's morning, he's roaming the meadow, and now maybe he's hearing something, looking up, wondering."

# *Adjusting Monty*

It would be easy to call Aaron Peterson a horse whisperer—easy and incorrect. Sure, he works with horses, but he likewise works with humans, dogs, even a bent-out-of-shape heifer on occasion. Furthermore, when he is engaging a horse, palpating its spine, wiggling its pelvis, massaging its massive jaw, he doesn't whisper. Over the course of an hour—an hour that tends to leave him sweaty and short of breath but also calm, loose, "emptied out"—he will hardly utter a word, at least not with his mouth.

"Horses don't speak English, obviously, but it does seem like they're very responsive to energy," Peterson said on a crisp November morning, pulling his truck off aptly named Sage Drive, north of Gunnison, Colorado, and parking between a barn and a fenced riding arena. He smoothed back his red ponytail, combed three fingers through his red beard. "The word *chiropractic* comes from the Greek for 'practice by hand.' I have to feel each horse in its body, as an individual—push the left-brain stuff to the side, all that conscious analysis of biomechanics, and respond with touch, you know?"

I didn't know. The science-art of adjusting Clydesdales and Andalusians—of improving their performance and, generally, their quality of life by "releasing sticky joints" and "clearing the system"—was way the hell off my radar. I told Peterson as much, employing a slightly more color-ful word than "hell," and he chuckled. "If I get to chatting with someone, and they learn what I do, I usually hear one of two responses," he said. "Either: You've got to be bull-shitting me. Or: Oh, fantastic, where are you based, can you come see my Nelly, she's been having some trouble with an inflamed hock."

Formerly a rock-climbing guide in California, Peter-son switched careers a number of years ago—traded cool gray granite under the palm for warm brown equine, as it were—and now has a private practice that keeps him trav-eling from stable to stable, all around Colorado. Exiting the truck, strolling across a gravel yard topped with thin patches of snow, I learned that he spends about a week on the Front Range each month, tending to a rotating clientele of Denver show horses, some of whom he's adjusted doz-ens of times. And what about this morning's appointment, I asked, deep in the heart of ranching country? "Travis Un-derwood is involved with animal rescue," he said. "I've met Monty twice before, but this will be the first we've seen each other since last spring."

On cue, a man outfitted exclusively in black Carhartt, save for his cowboy boots, stepped from the barn, lead rope in hand, one thousand pounds of elegant power—or pow-erful elegance—trailing behind. "Monty was one of twenty highbred Arabians trapped down in Arizona, locked in a stall for eight years, almost totally neglected," Underwood said by way of introduction. "He's got a club foot and it messes with his gait." Peterson patted Monty's flank, adding, "Their hooves are incredibly important. I try to have a global mentality, but I do pay a lot of attention to the feet."

Our parade of four entered the riding arena via a dented metal gate, Underwood tickling Monty's twitchy nose, cooing at him, calling him "goofball." Peterson stood to the side for a minute, observing, then came in close, lightly placing both hands on Monty's withers. "He wouldn't let a vet hang out there," Underwood said. "Monty hates needles. But this, this feels good, eh, boy?"

And so it began—a fluid sequence of stances, positions, pressures, pinches, stretches, shakes, tugs, tweaks. Picture a kid playing with the utmost intention and professionalism on a mammalian jungle gym. Better yet, if it's possible, imagine a kind of nonsexual tour of the *Kama Sutra*, bodies twining and untwining, spinning slow circles, silvery breath-clouds rising in the clear autumn air. Peterson gripped a leg and gave a quick whip, as one might a tablecloth or bedsheet. With the aid of a dense foam block—his only instrument—he gained enough height to administer CPR pumps of a sort to Monty's lofty hip. Fingers busied themselves with croup, gaskin, shoulder, knee.

More interesting than the dynamics of this interspecies dance though was a certain underlying stillness—the stillness that characterizes intense focus, immersive concentration. Specifically, I was drawn to Peterson's semiglazed eyes, which were on the ground, on distant buttes, on a turkey vulture overhead, on everything besides Monty. Practice of the hand indeed! The dialogue here wasn't just nonverbal, it was largely nonvisual. As for Monty's eyes, they were "sleepy-soft," according to Underwood—a sign, like the Elvis lip-curl and rumbling belly, that he was relaxed.

Having checked the "occiput and atlas," scanned for "vertebral subluxation complexes," conjured a resounding *pop* from who knows what ligament, and dodged a few innocent kicks, Peterson concluded the adjustment with what appeared, despite its assuredly technical function, to be nothing more than a friendly hug around the neck. "Go to your pooping corner," Underwood said, his tone that of an encouraging father, and Monty burst toward a mound of sun-dried horse apples on the far side of the arena. The mound got bigger. Peterson smiled.

"I enjoy doing humans, but I really love doing horses," he told me after we'd said our goodbyes and hopped into the truck. "With humans there are these layers of psychology, this onion that you have to peel. I can tell a horse that his healing depends on accepting Allah, Jesus, Buddha, whoever, but the horse won't care. What matters to a horse is physical, direct. It's a cleaner line of communication."

Peterson smoothed his ponytail, unaware that, like Monty's tangled black mane, it now held a quantity of yellow hay.

"But don't get me wrong," he said. "I only vaguely speak horse."

~    ~    ~

HITHER AND YON

# The Atlas

It's always like this. I knock, they come out smiling, we hug, briefly discuss the weather, the news, baseball, my drive—and then an atlas appears on the dining room table, alongside roasted almonds, glasses of water or soda or beer. I'm not exaggerating: It's *always* like this. The food and drink, but that's incidental. What I mean is the atlas.

For ten years, I've been showing up on their doorstep, dirty and sore from adventures in baking arroyos and blinding snowfields. The doorstep has moved—they used to live in Grand Junction, Colorado, on the Western Slope, and now they live in Windsor, Colorado, on the Great Plains—but little else has changed. Ten years of the road-weary me and the welcoming them. Ten years of the table and the atlas. Ten years of this conversation that roams from Juneau to Tucson to Taos Pueblo to Yellowstone and beyond.

Who are these people, these geographers? There are different ways of answering the question. They are my great-aunt and great-uncle. They are a girl on a farm during the Depression and a boy backpacking into the wilderness prior to its designation as "Wilderness." They are Jeanne, age ninety-one, who recently published a novel, and George, also ninety-one, a former Forest Service entomologist. She's intrigued by Burning Man. He jogs six miles at dawn. Open, engaged, vibrant—they are my mentors.

Okay, fair enough. But here's another way of answering the question: *They are the atlas.*

Before heading to bed, we talk for five hours, pages fanning, words crossing thousands of miles: the Missouri's headwater streams, the Chiricahua's bird-loud canyons. At breakfast, our fingers resume where they left off, tracing lines between counties and states, between *this* phase of life and *that* phase of life. The 1950s, Alaska and seals. The 1960s, California and sequoias. By 1971 they were in Golden, Colorado, flank of the Front Range. By 1991 they were retired, cruising Arizona's White Mountains and New Mexico's San Juan Basin, home a fifth-wheel trailer.

Says one of them, passing the almonds: *If you happen to be going down the Moki Dugway…*

Says the other, refilling my empty glass: *That reminds me of getting invited into this rancher's parlor to tour his collection of…*

Is there anywhere my great-aunt and great-uncle haven't been, any pictograph panel or podunk library they haven't spent a day enjoying? Nonagenarians often mistaken for septuagenarians, their minds are snappy, their cumulative experience vast. Elk antlers, potsherds, rutted BLM two-tracks, moods and moments, places and places and places: Indeed, *they are the atlas.*

Or perhaps that's a bit misleading. In a sense, the atlas is its own person, a fourth talker at the table. Gathered around, bumping elbows, leaning close, we listen to *its* stories of jackrabbits, rainstorms, monuments commemorating massacres, ice cream shops in dusty towns, unanticipated beauty.

Says something, some voice: *If you're lucky and catch it on a winter afternoon, the shadows here will slant…*

Time pauses under this spell of topographies and toponyms, age vanishes, and we three become equals in wonder, in curiosity, in the desire to light out for the territories once again, once again, once again. The West, it seems, is too deep to fathom, too broad to traverse. The West, it seems, is infinite.

Really, I find myself thinking, is there anywhere they wouldn't love to go, these geographers, these mentors, these trailblazers? Given an extra couple decades, given a slug from the Fountain of Youth, is there any opportunity they wouldn't seize, any rock they wouldn't put their shared weight against, tilt upright, and peek beneath just because?

Oh, but time—it can't stop itself from running. The atlas falls shut and age returns. Standing in the driveway, our visit over, we briefly discuss the weather, my route, and then with a hug I'm launched. Gas pedal pressed. Unsure when I'll be back.

I have to assume that Jeanne and George, who are sixty years my senior, will die before I do, will blaze that dim trail as they have countless trails already. I have to assume that eventually they will go and I will stay and that my staying will resemble motion, the same old wanderlust. I have to assume a ratty sleeping bag and pavement beneath spinning tires. I have to assume the continued need for a doorstep, a friendly greeting, a dozen almonds, a cold drink.

In this imagined future, I see myself more alone on earth yet also less alone. The atlas, the completely ordinary atlas, the magical atlas, the atlas that is spirit and possibility and exploration and every type of dirt and sky, every type of feeling, everything that counts, everything simultaneously: The atlas will remain.

Maybe they'll bequeath it to me in their will? I'd like to have such a thing available for my grandnephew, that eager traveler of the distant future, should he ever need a hand getting oriented in the world.

# Wild Reading

On April 26, 1336, the poet-scholar Francesco Petrarch climbed Mont Ventoux, in Provence, for "harmless pleasure." Reaching the summit, he didn't wrap himself in a warm cloak, gobble some crusty bread, and stare dumbly into the blue distance, as one might expect of an exhausted bushwhacker. Rather, he cracked a copy of St. Augustine's *Confessions*—that "handy little book"—and filled his mind with text. The excursion may have been the birth of modern hiking, but it was also an early instance of another outdoorsy pastime.

For years I've been intrigued by wilderness reading, asking myself the *meaning* of lugging literature into the backcountry. What was going on there atop Mont Ventoux? What's going on each time a Kindle sneaks into the kit? And why did I once allow David Foster Wallace's 1,079-page novel *Infinite Jest* to ride my achy back like some kind of evil monkey for two straight weeks? It was waterlogged from having been fumbled into a stream. It was splotchy with mold. It was...*welcomed*?

Sleeping bag, stove, iodine tablets, Swiss Army knife, extra socks—sure, these items are useful on a backpacking adventure. But books? Do they deepen our immersion in

place? Do they distract us from place? Really, what's the
deal with that evil monkey?

~

I first contemplated this subject at age nineteen, while trekking solo from Denver to Durango on the Colorado Trail.
New to the West, disturbed by the aridity and vastness, I
decided to meet the strange region with as little mediation
as possible. Like any proper ounce-counting minimalist,
I carried the barest essentials: bivvy sack in lieu of a tent,
scavenged-twig chopsticks in lieu of a metal spoon. Need-
less to say, Emily Dickinson and Plato stayed home.

The forests were oddly unpeopled that August, and I
regularly found myself in the company of solemn spruce
and brooks that failed to babble. Without human voices rising from the page, offering me conversation and comfort,
I grew lonely, edgy. By the end of the third week, my supplies were dwindling and I was ravenous for Belgian waffles,
Klondike bars, conversation, dumb jokes, *Sports Illustrated*,
scripture, whatever. A cute blond bibliophile toting a ruck-
sack of Melville, Snickers, Twain, and Doritos would have
proved that wishes can come true, but a gruff miner-dude
with an eighty-word lexicon and a case of cheap beer would
have been agreeable too.

And then, as I crossed a dirt road beneath drizzly morning skies, what should appear but a rusty pickup? The truck
slowed at the sight of my raised thumb and I hopped in.
*Please, sir, drop me at the nearest supermarket. Is there a used
bookshop in town?*

That evening, having gorged on junk food and, more im-
portantly, acquired a tattered paperback for fifty cents, I returned to the cold, rainy mountains. My headlamp's beam

locked onto a biography of Mozart—and refused to let go. Here was the Sawatch Range enfolded in storm, some of the tallest peaks in the lower forty-eight, and here, also, was bustling Vienna, *Eine kleine Nachtmusik*, the life and times of Wolfgang Amadeus.

Never before had I devoured nonfiction with such a ferocious appetite. Six hours and twelve chapters later, eyes burning, I passed out, only to rise at dawn, hoist my pack, and hit the trail. The spring in my step made it clear that literature can serve as a kind of fuel for the solitary walker. Like instant coffee and oatmeal, it gave me the strength to push on.

Which leads to another aspect of reading outdoors: What to bring? Dehydrated pea soup? Pepperoni? Wordsworth? Toni Morrison?

Occasionally the answer is easy—think of Muir's *My First Summer in the Sierra* for a Yosemite pack trip, Powell's *The Exploration of the Colorado River and Its Canyons* for a Grand Canyon float. More often than not, though, the possibilities overwhelm a nerd like me. The Tetons with Mardy Murie are not the Tetons with Isaac Asimov, and the Owens Valley with Mary Austin is not the Owens Valley with Roger Tory Peterson, Kurt Vonnegut, or Geoffrey Chaucer.

Cut to the foggy gray beaches of Washington's Olympic Peninsula, a thin strip of sand bordered by nearly impenetrable rainforest on one side and wholly impenetrable ocean—ranks of tiered breakers—on the other. A couple years had passed since the Colorado Trail (spiritual bike tours with Bashō and Thomas Merton, an arduous winter expedition with Sir Ernest Shackleton) and I was again tromping solo, hoping that a spell at the continent's intense edge might…

Well, I didn't know what I was hoping for, actually. Perhaps it was visceral contact, the tang of salt in my soup. Perhaps it was an elemental scouring, a cleansing of too many months spent indoors worrying about fame, glory, power, and how to pay the rent, how to afford pinto beans. In either case, I figured that Kerouac's *Big Sur*, with its Pacific coast vibes, would make for suitable bedtime snuggling.

Turns out I was wrong, quite wrong. Lying in my damp, gritty tent, mere paces from the thrashing water, I discovered that *Big Sur* documents Kerouac's descent into alcoholic insanity, what his pal Ginsberg described as "paranoiac confusion." Furthermore, the story culminates with a dissonant aural hallucination, a poem that is essentially the author's inebriated ear submerged in surf, fishing for lyrics.

"Josh—coof—patra— / Aye ee mo powsh—"

Um, beg pardon?

"Ssst—Cum here read me— / Dirty postcard—Urchin sea— / Karash your name—?"

Where the Mozart biography had pulled me back from the brink—had given me the companionship I needed to keep going on the trail—the Kerouac forced me into an inhuman chaos of waves. For five days I stumbled through frothing foam and mazes of mist, encountering nobody but seals and crabs, and for five nights I listened to eerie techno-symphonies, bickering mermaids, the incessant rush and rip of tides.

In a sense, *Big Sur* was the ideal book, an echo of the ocean's severe strangeness. But "ideal" is after-the-fact talk, armchair-philosopher talk. During the hike, I was immersed, in over my head, frantically swimming. At three a.m., tossing and turning, dreaming that I was drowning, I would have given anything for the dry, soothing logic of a vacuum's manual.

~

An urge toward language is surely integral to our identity as *Homo sapiens*—"the animal who possesses speech," as Aristotle put it. Erudite scholars could no doubt trace this idea—the significance of possessing speech and, in turn, of being possessed *by* speech—through Western intellectual history and beyond, to the very evolutionary origins of our species.

I am not an erudite scholar, just a guy with worn leather boots and an eagerness to ramble through canyonlands, alphabets, varied terrains. The best I can offer is obvious: Reading in the wilderness isn't easily reduced to good or bad, this or that. Books lead us to an enriched sense of our surroundings, yes, but they also help us escape the elemental present. They function in countless ways, providing botanical detail, local lore, critiques of the status quo, visions of the future, entertainment when you're socked in by blizzards, arcane wisdom, wigged fellows tinkling pianos in Vienna, maddening oceans. Bundled in a dirty fleece jacket, they even make for a decent, albeit firm, pillow.

If you'll excuse the pun, the question of wild reading is itself an open book, an invitation to speculate and, better yet, to experiment.

My experiments of late are less concerned with how literature shapes appreciation of places than with the inverse: how *places* shape appreciation of *literature*. Specifically, I've developed a Sunday afternoon practice of browsing classical Chinese landscape poetry in the thick woods bordering my rural home. According to certain commentators, the vivid imagery of a Wang Wei verse—light falling on a bed of jade-green moss, a crimson leaf floating circles in a river's eddy—*enacts* the movement of nature. That is, instead of describing the ceaseless burgeoning forth of organic reality, the poem literally re-creates that dynamic, lines lifting from the white space, expanding in the mind, disappearing into silence.

For me, an hour chilling with Wang Wei is all about the encompassing scene, about it *animating* the book in my lap. Sitting on a shadow-dappled log, my attention flickers between warblers and words, and I notice a parallel motion. These intricate markings on the page...they're flying? These letters...they're birds to read? Language seems earthly, of a piece with the environment.

At such moments I feel a surging unity, as if the animal who possesses speech belongs here among the wild energies of wild country. Poetry in a dim study—dusty shelves, leather chairs, windows closed—isn't the same. Wrong habitat. Almost like reading in a zoo.

# Nature-Loving Beards

You know Henry Thoreau. He built a shack at Walden Pond, planted beans, read some books, communed with woodchucks and thunderstorms. His beard is sort of funny—most images I've seen show him with an Amish-style chinstrap—but I've put him on the list anyway. You've got to put Henry on the list.

Next comes John Muir. His beard's reputation precedes him, so I will curb my urge to praise. I like to picture the two of them—the beard and the man—rambling for weeks on end in the High Sierra. When dusk falls they wrap themselves up and hunker down, sheltering one another. They carry no tent, no sleeping bag.

Walt Whitman once wrote, "I think I could turn and live with animals." Does he mean the squirrels and chickadees and hornets nesting beneath his Adam's apple? Surely his beard was a habitat, an ecosystem, a world teeming with multifarious life, like the world described in his poems.

Most folks probably remember John Wesley Powell as the mutton-chopped, one-armed, river-running hardman who explored the Grand Canyon in 1869, but I am partial to what his chops became in the 1880s, when they were allowed to freely and unabashedly roam across his face. Think Gimli, the dwarf from *The Lord of the Rings*. Think big.

It'd be nice to give Chuck Darwin a shout. Unfortunately, this list is exclusively for homegrown beards, and dumb rules must be taken very, very seriously. As an indirect homage, we might turn our attention to writer John Burroughs, a Darwinian doppelganger if there ever was one. In a photo I found on the internet, his beard seems to have sprouted a second beard, a spur-beard of sorts, and though it's unlikely, a part of me thinks it's Chuck's beard risen from the grave, visiting, hanging out, chatting about whatever it is beards chat about.

Sorry, friends, no beard on Teddy Roosevelt, just a 'stache, but one so important to North American conservation that it deserves brief mention. Sometimes, when I'm drifting off at night, when dreams are close, I see it creeping over the lands it dearly loved, a bristly caterpillar crossing the Great Plains, ascending the Rockies, inching through the Yosemite Valley, heading west into the setting sun.

What of Ansel Adams? Personally, I think he made a wise decision when he went bald. That's not to say his beard wasn't handsome early on—trim, black, a few dignified streaks of gray—but consider the competition, the nature-loving beards it was up against. Volume? Mass? Square footage? Forget about it. When contrasted with that round, shiny dome, though, it's hard to miss.

Let it be clearly stated that a list of such discernment and penetrating insight as the one you are presently reading doesn't magically, effortlessly appear while imbibing numerous dark beers on a Friday evening. Did Bob Marshall—Adirondack peakbagger, founder of the Wilderness

Society—even have a beard? His is not a famous visage, but I did some searching. While Bobby was clean-shaven much of the time, when out in the backcountry his beard got busy. Points awarded for bushiness, twigginess, and—à la Ansel—it being longer than the hair atop his head.

Edward Abbey, a.k.a. Cactus Ed, a.k.a. Mr. Scraggly, is yet another example of beard-man hybridization—and spirit too. When I've sat too stolidly at the computer, when I sense my soul withering and puckering and curling at the edges, I listen for the voice behind the hair. Get outside, the voice shouts. It's full of piss and vinegar and sandstone and desert sky and adoration of all things wild, free, uncut, unkempt.

By now you've probably noticed that there's something missing from this list, and really, I do feel bad about it. Here's the problem: Most women don't grow beards, ample or otherwise. I studied damn near fifty photos of Rachel Carson, shots from all angles, in all types of light, and never in her life, whether as a young marine biologist or as a grandmotherly hawk-saving badass, did she sport even the wispiest of goatees. The same can be said for Susan Fenimore Cooper, Mary Austin, Mary Oliver, Ann Zwinger, Annie Dillard, Ellen Meloy, and countless other forceful, tender, inspiring writers. So, in solidarity with these literary heroes of mine, and to emphasize that it is not the face but rather the beating heart that loves our precious earthly abode, I hereby lather my jaw. After many months of slow growth, yes, the time has at last arrived to shave the patchy sucker off.

# Things I Will Not Say
## about Wilderness

I will not say that wilderness is a tonic, balm, or medicine for the troubled soul; that most everyone has a troubled soul in need of moss's healing touch and birdsong's rejuvenating cheeriness; that this common soul-ache is just a little human-sized sliver of despair situated within the broader soul of the natural world; that I have walked for weeks among meadows and outcrops and waterfalls, blisters on my toes, a grin spreading from ear to ear and beyond.

I will not say that trees speak; that their leafy words have offered me solace in moments of pain and their branchy words pointed me in the appropriate direction when I was lost; that at the Grand Canyon, while telling a friend how I sincerely appreciated pinyon pines, the realization hit me like a ton of glorious bricks that a nearby pinyon pine was listening; that alone, backpacking in the Rockies, I once curled myself beneath a venerable bristlecone, closed my eyes, opened them again, and was granted by the tree a waking dream in which I saw something akin to the face of the divine, a face that looked like bark.

I will not say that lying on your back at dusk beside a tarn where frogs chorus to the rising moon is a definite must; that if you do choose to recline in such a locale the moon will carry your thoughts into the sky until those thoughts are no longer yours; that the frogs, unperturbed, will go on chorusing their froggy chorus; that eventually the moon will set, carrying the former *you* with it into darkness.

I will not say that time is a polished pebble easily lifted, considered, and dropped into the stream by the edge of the trail to sit forever under clear flowing water; that this stream is itself a pebble some older being previously lifted, considered, and dropped; that pebbles and streams when taken together are, as the saying goes, like "turtles all the way down"; that if one's not careful preparing dinner at the campsite, a pebble can find its way into the soup, the soup whose broth is water from the stream.

I will not say that the Stanislaus National Forest, on the Sierra Nevada's western slope, is in fact owned only by itself and beholden only to itself; that the more we try to claim places rather than hum with places, whether the Everglades, the North Cascades, or an anonymous patch of dirt and weeds in Altoona, Kansas, the more we lose a thing gladly and freely given; that the loss of a thing gladly and freely given forebodes a parallel loss in the collective body of humanity; that the more we lose gladness and freeness, the more we reach and grasp and claim and, well, suck.

I will not say that canoe guide Sigurd Olson was right when he wrote, "There is a penalty for too much comfort and ease, a penalty of lassitude and inertia and the frustrated feeling that goes with unreality"; that eleventh-century Chinese landscape painter Kuo Hsi was correct when he said, "The din of the dusty world and the locked-in-ness of human habitations are what human nature habitually abhors"; that desert rambler Ellen Meloy nailed the nail squarely on its head when she forged her voice into a hammer and professed, "There are people who have no engaged conversation with the land whatsoever, no sense of its beauty or extremes"; that the aforementioned succeeded in coming anywhere close to the eloquence that is rain on palms, a coyote glancing up from the kill, the calcium in a snail's shell, dry wind across stiff brown grass, et cetera.

Wrapping up, I will not say that I trust human phrases, inky scratches, the tongue's ribbony cursive scribbles, or anything remotely of their ilk to accurately express the many truths that I know with absolute certainty in my mute heart, in my inarticulate bones, to be utterly, awesomely, incontrovertibly, truthfully true.

# Addressing the Forces That Would
# Destroy Us and Everything We Love

You might think you've got time. Let me be the first to tell you: It's a lie. Yeah, you'll coast on fumes for a decade or a century, take down more forests, suck up more groundwater, spread a bit more suffering here and there, but it's fumes you're running on, mere fumes. Your back is to the wall. The wall is a ticking clock. Your days are numbered.

I get it, you've been reading about yourself, hooray for you. Your head is big, inflated with photos and headlines. I saw one this morning and I'll admit to tasting the fear, the fear like metal in the mouth, like the moment before you vomit, like the barrel of a gun. It was something about swans. It was something about shallow graves. It was this and that, gloom and doom. It was some little something about plastics, whales, mosses, winters.

But let me show you something different. Come here. Look at this guy. He leads people into the sandstone canyons and the high cold mountain cirques and the aspen groves where pale white trunks float ghostly in the moonlight. And then he leaves them there, leaves these people with no food, no books, no toys, no distractions. He leaves them with just a water jug and the clothes on their animal bodies, with just the wild animals of the land and the wild animals of the mind.

Watch these people. Watch them sit and wait, wait and sit. Maybe every once in a while some old terror or old joy brings them to their feet, some lightning or rockfall or inching insect or green glowing eye. Watch them run circles in place until they are exhausted and sure to collapse, and then, yes, watch them dance. Watch them push on past collapse and into the night and through the glorious dawn and farther still.

Your clock is ticking. Your days are numbered. Meanwhile, they're still out there. They hum and pile pebbles. They squint at the grass with their ears and attend to the wind with their noses and sniff the soil with the tips of their fingers. They hang in there, these simple people, hang in there through boredom and fear and pain, through conversations with lichens and figures in the clouds and rain that rips dreams. They sleep. They wake. They do not eat and they hang in there, crying tears for a vision, for a way to go forward with bolder, longer steps and a stronger, redder heart. They hang. They cry. They sleep and sway and keep crying, crying, crying for the loss of what is already lost, what was left behind when they followed this guy I know away from the roads, deep into the canyons and the mountains and the forests of pale ghostly trees.

So do you understand what I'm saying? Tick-tock, tick-tock. The hour is late. I'm saying that you can have those species you're set on taking. You can have the groundwater. Here, take the climate. Take the moss, the river, the swans. Take the flight from the wings and the freeze from the ice. I'm feeling expansive. I'm in a generous mood. Have fun while it lasts. Read about yourself. But listen. Hear that? Tick-tock, tick-tock.

And listen: Everything will change and nothing will change. As always. We are made of remembering and you are made of forgetting.

You're laughing. You're saying the only word you speak, the drip of poison. I get it.

But come close. Look. I know this guy, this guy who leads people into a wilderness that can't be destroyed. I know these people. You should meet them.

## Write-Ins for President

I elect that bull elk in the Snake River.

I elect that raven in Canyonlands National Park.

I elect autumn moonlight on metal roofs.

I elect the strand of barbed wire that fell from the post and is now woven into the tall brown grass.

I elect the tall brown grass.

I elect my neighbors' cat—the neighbors who are always cursing one another and screaming hateful things—because every morning he sits with me on the fire escape and watches the sunrise without meowing a single word.

I elect the feeling of boots laced tight.

I elect potatoes cooked however.

I elect the valley of my birth and its faded, sagging, leaning, crooked-in-the-best-sense-of-the-word barns.

I elect rain improvising songs on a busted junkyard piano.

I elect the ghost of my grandfather, Dean, because the man never wanted to be anything but a farmer, so says my grandmother, Betty.

I elect my grandmother, Betty, because at ninety-five she takes the long view.

I elect the *thump-thump-thump* of many wagging tails.

I elect the hungry mouse who stole my snack but did so honestly, out in the open.

I elect that dream my sister once had of a black bear hurtling through our childhood house, breaking through a bathroom window, transforming midair into a timber wolf, climbing higher and higher into the nighttime sky, higher and higher, and higher, and higher, and then falling as a brilliant shooting star.

I elect that dream I once had of a monkey riding a flying goat, a dream in which I understood intuitively, instantly, that a monkey riding a flying goat foretells the healing of all wounds.

I elect the tears on my cheeks when I woke up.

I elect the Kaibab Plateau.

I elect crushed mint.

I elect snowflakes on spiderwebs.

I elect littered napkins folded together by the wind and placed, as if by magic, at the base of a street-corner trash can.

I elect a climb of Precarious Peak that made me, and will forever keep me, humble as a pebble.

I elect our innate mammalian ability to walk one hundred miles, hardly eating, hardly sleeping, at home in the weather, whatever weather.

I elect that which can't be written in, that which will guide us forward, ever forward, regardless of who lives in some white mansion.

# Talking Clouds

Last week, when I swung by the assisted living facility for a quick hello, Gram surprised me with the news that she had been a good Catholic girl from Yonkers—the Irish Lass from the Big City—and that she had maintained her chastity right up to her very wedding night. Is news the appropriate word for such a disclosure? Being her grandson, I was slightly put off by this saucy talk and suggested that we pour ourselves some ginger ale in little clear plastic cups and head to the patio, where we could talk weather instead.

At ninety-five years old, Gram likes the weather, no doubt about it. Specifically, she likes the clouds that are the weather's heart and soul—how they flop around in the sky, how they hang on the empty blue. These are her words, an uncommon and delightful music that issues from dementia. She doesn't talk cirrus or stratus or cumulonimbus, and she doesn't say, *I see an elephant,* or, *That one resembles a ship with three sails,* or, *Hey, wow, it's a monster with a long tail.* No, when Gram talks clouds she talks about the clouds themselves: shape and motion, pattern and texture, two drifting together, a third drifting away, a fourth pausing, a fifth disappearing.

White can have so many different whites inside of its whiteness, she said last week.

Indeed, I replied, refilling our little clear plastic cups.

Gram likes talking weather, no doubt about it, and Gram likes talking Granddad too—a nice quiet man, the Protestant Farm Boy from Illinois who grew up to marry the Irish Lass from the Big City. He was one of the first commercial pilots and she was one of the first commercial stewardesses, and it was the Golden Age of Aviation. They met in Newfoundland when their flights were grounded by storms, and it was the Golden Age of Aviation. They met again months later, in the Azores, and it was the Golden Age of Aviation, the Golden Age of Aviation.

A kind man who didn't complain about anything, Gram told me last week, until that one day when he said, *I don't feel quite right*, and by Friday afternoon he was gone.

He was great, I said. I loved climbing into his lap and "helping" with crossword puzzles.

Did you ever meet him? she asked in response.

Dementia, according to the experts, is a kind of cloud. Okay. But planes cut through clouds and, no doubt about it, Gram likes talking planes as well—how their contrails swoosh and swish, how they hang on the empty blue. Planes carry us to Newfoundland, to the Azores, to the man of our dreams. Planes transport us to lands we've never visited and lands we've forgotten and lands we can just make out at the receding edge of memory.

Sitting on the patio at the assisted living facility last week, sipping our little clear plastic cups of ginger ale, I learned, as I had learned the week prior, that young folks better label the backs of their photographs, because it's easy to lose track of where and when and the rest, and that young folks should likewise label their shirts and pants, because things are bound to get lost at a place like this.

A place like this, I thought. What is a place like this? Isn't it a regular place, a place beneath the sky that touches all places?

Here comes another cloud, Gram said. This one's in a hurry. Watch now. I think it's going to catch the others. Give it a minute. Give it a minute. Watch now and let's see what it does.

I did as instructed: I watched.

Look at that one, Gram continued, pointing with the hand that held the little clear plastic cup, raising a toast without knowing she was raising a toast, without any awareness whatsoever that she was celebrating the sky that touches all places, the sky that touches the tops of all clouds.

Yeah, look at that one, I echoed.

Her face, round and wrinkled, seemed to glow from the inside. That one sure does like to flop, she said. Flopping around. Flopping around without a care. Would you believe that?

# *Ways to Take Your Coffee*

With snow falling on blue spruce and a cardinal's red quickness at the feeder and the fireplace's crackly warmth easing into your bones and the final pages of a book about bears and the opening pages of a book about monks and no plans for the morning, the afternoon, tomorrow, the rest of your life.

With a frisky dog straining against the leash and then released from the leash and then running frisky-wild, frisky-free, high on the caffeine that is canine living, that is a meadow of tall grass rich with secret smells and plentiful muck and perfect spots for rolling.

With ancient mountains all around and an entire ancient mountain beneath your butt and the climb still burning your legs and the climb still thrilling your mind and clouds building on the horizon, a storm coming for sure, but you've got time, you and your best friend, plenty of time to light the stove and brew a strong pot and trade sips while two golden eagles circle, circle, circle the summit, never once flapping their wings.

With a splash of whiskey after an incredibly long weekend of whiskey and maybe some nature documentaries on the tube, maybe a greasy egg sandwich, certainly a head-ache, a rock-splitting headache, definitely the couch.

With the tray table lowered and the flight attendant of-fering refills and the plane sort of empty, nobody in your row, nobody between you and that thirty-thousand-foot view of twisty rivers, lumpy hills, entire watersheds, the earth just going and going, no end in sight.

With bare feet in cool sand and the surf whispering along the beach and five gray whales spouting in the distance where millions of tiny silver fish turn as one, flash as one in the oneness of ocean, the oceanic oneness that comes up to your ankles, your shins, your knees, then pulls back into the immensity of itself like an invitation, like a dare.

With tired, bearded men in a desert truck stop at mid-night and then on out to your old trusty car and then on down the old lonely road, basins and ranges, ranges and ba-sins, the radio off because it's broken, the pedal pressed, the tires whumping, the sky without stars, a bottomless cup, so black, so black, no cream, no sugar.

# Doe's Song

Jennifer hit the deer and the deer came onto the windshield and the deer fell to the pavement. The deer got up and tried to run but the deer couldn't run and fell to the pavement. The deer's front left leg was broken, flipped over one shoulder like a scarf. The deer got up and ran on three legs across the road, the bad leg dangling. The whole thing took maybe thirty seconds, a minute tops.

Mike and I were following Jennifer in a second car and when she slammed the brakes we slammed the brakes. We saw the deer try to stand and we saw the deer fall and we saw the deer rise and run. We saw the leg. She was a doe, not sure what age. It's obvious that she was lovely, but I'll say it anyway: She was lovely. Brown and slim. Smooth. If she had a name, no human knew it.

This was springtime, a soft evening in Princeton, New Jersey, a narrow road in forested suburbs, the kind of place where deer are hit every day. I will repeat that: the kind of place where deer are hit every day. I will repeat that: every day. Where every day deer are struck with the force of rockfall and lightning. Where roads curve and bones litter green thickets separating elegant mansions. Where we live our lives, always moving, always rushing this way and that, here and there. Where spots of blood on new leaves go mostly unnoticed and kids can be heard laughing in their yards, playing after the homework is done.

Yes, a soft evening, the clouds rosy, the sky between the clouds a pale, delicate blue.

When I reached Jennifer's window she was sobbing, face in her hands. "Did you see the leg?" she said, the hands coming down to her lap, thin and red, her face red and wet. "Did you see the leg? Is it going to be okay?" I assumed that the doe would not be okay. I assumed that the doe was in a tremendous amount of pain. "It happened so fast. There wasn't anything I could do. Is it going to be okay? Is it going to die?" I didn't know. I was thinking of suffering. "Is it going to be okay?"

Cars were lining up behind us, cars and more cars. I waved them around, crossed the road, and there she was, fifty feet into the woods, curled on the ground, looking at me, shaking. I stopped, not wanting to scare her, and said I was a friend. Unsure what else to do, I sang a little song, a gentle tune without words. I invented the song as I went, the doe looking at me, shaking, a sadness thickening in my body. And then something cut through that sadness. Cleaved that sadness. I stepped back. I knew for certain that my presence was only making things worse.

Sure enough, the doe got up and ran, the bad leg now like a sock of pennies.

Returning to the scene of the accident, I found Mike in the passenger seat, Jennifer gripping the steering wheel. They weren't talking and they weren't crying. They were mesmerized, it seemed, by the dashboard's dust. A pickup truck passed behind me, way too fast and way too close. I

felt the press of air against my neck, the force of it, the hint
of rockfall and lightning.

"Do you think it will be okay? Do you think it will live?"

Mike stared ahead, scrutinized the dust. I said nothing.
Jennifer raised her thin red hands and dropped her face to
meet them.

⁓

Richard Nelson's 1997 book, *Heart and Blood: Living with
Deer in America,* doesn't deal extensively with roadkill,
but the few statistics it does provide are overwhelming. By
chance, I had been overwhelmed with them at breakfast,
drinking my coffee, reading at the table in Vermont prior to
getting in the car for the drive to New Jersey.

"Back in 1961 when deer were scarce by present stan-
dards," Nelson writes, "official reports counted fewer than
400 deer killed by cars on [Wisconsin's] roads. Just 30 years
later, in the 1990s, the number had soared to between 35,000
and 50,000 whitetails killed annually, and the actual figure
could be much higher, since injured deer often get away
from the highway before dying."

He goes on: "The number of deer killed by cars in Boulder [Colorado] varies from 120 to more than 200 each year,
and an equal number (if not more) are injured or straggle
off to die in the brushland. Deer accidents increase during
winter, midsummer, and especially the fall rut. An animal
control officer told me, 'We'll pick up two or three dead deer
every day in rutting season, plus usually one more that's injured so badly it has to be euthanized.'"

Spring morning, a cup of coffee, the house quiet. I re-
clined in my chair and thought through the math. Boulder
plus Colorado's other cities, towns, and open roads. Plus

Wisconsin. Plus Florida and California. Plus Vermont and New Jersey. *Two or three. Plus usually one more. Between 35,000 and 50,000. Could be much higher.* I took a gulp, then took another. *Straggle off to die in the brushland.*

If all went well, I'd make it to Princeton in five hours, perhaps faster.

Seven years ago I drove from Vermont to Colorado keeping a tally, organized by species, on the inside cover of an atlas. The atlas sat in the passenger seat with a pencil atop it, one of those short pencils you find in libraries. For some two thousand miles it was just me and the road and the dead animals and the tally and the short pencil. The radio in my car was busted. No air-conditioning either.

The first day's push got me to Lansing, Michigan, where an old best friend lived at the time. We hadn't seen each other in years, so we drank late into the night, joking and remembering and playing guitars. I didn't mention my tally, the early doe in the Adirondacks, the second with her neck snapped back, the skunk whose white stripe was red, the mash of porcupine, the smears I couldn't name. Ohio was bad, worse than New York. A red-tailed hawk with its wing sticking straight up. A stain that looked like tar.

Morning came too early, hot and hungover, and in no time I was on the road again. My destination was Chicago, a half-day's drive at most. Within fifteen minutes, though, I began to doubt whether I would make it that far. It was the raccoons, *Procyon lotor.* It was the damn tally. It was me picking the pencil up, putting it down, picking it up, putting it down, picking it up. I knew I'd feel better if I stopped counting, but I wouldn't let myself stop counting. I was thirsty and ran out of water. I worried that I might vomit. When I finally hit Chicago, my shirt was off and I was sweating and the vinyl seat was sucking against my aching spine. I'd racked up an even twenty raccoons, three deer, a squirrel, and four unidentifiables.

Iowa. Nebraska. The rest of the trip was more of the same, though never quite as low and sad and hard as Michigan. This is a big country, and it gets bigger when you're watching and tallying and grabbing the pencil again and again. You know that kind of pencil I'm talking about, the kind from libraries? They don't have an eraser. Any mark you make with one of those pencils is a mark made for good.

❧

There was a game on, the Philadelphia 76ers. I don't really care for pro basketball, but Mike and Jennifer like sports, and I was their guest, so we watched. We also prepared a feast. Jennifer made tortilla chips from scratch with lots of oil and salt. I chopped jalapeños and onions, cooked black beans and rice. Mike grated cheddar cheese and fed the dog, Lucy. We had some beers. Jennifer had red wine. Nobody mentioned the deer.

The game was close and long and the commercials came and came like the raccoons that morning heading west from Lansing. They felt to me like dead things, like little flashy, noisy corpses. I sat on the carpeted floor, a giant pillow propped against the base of the couch for a backrest. We had some ice cream. Another drink. Three-pointer, slam dunk. During a commercial break I went out to the driveway and looked at the stars. I went out again during the next commercial. And the next. We talked for a while about nothing in particular, relaxed and played with Lucy, said goodnight and went to bed.

Edging up to sleep, I saw the stars inside my eyes, constellations bordering dreams.

The next day, rising before dawn to get the coffee started, I found Jennifer sitting on the couch, wrapped in a blanket, her face red and wet and buried in her hands, the hands lifted to meet her face.

～

At the Little Otter Creek Wildlife Management Area, in Ferrisburgh, Vermont, I discovered the spot where the deer that die on nearby roads get piled, though I'm not sure whose job it is to haul them there. It's a mass grave and an open grave on a dead-end track in a stand of white pine. The smell drags you along the track, the curious horror of that smell, and then you see a leg. Then another. Then the shallow depression with the skulls and tangled bodies, the stages of decay, the churn and grind of time. Often I've sat on the ground and forced myself to be still, to inhale, to look. The stink is dire. Teeth and jawbones are everywhere. This is a mile from my childhood house, an easy walk.

I've got a hunch few people know the grave exists besides me and the person who hauls the bodies from the road.

～

When I was a teenager, I spent a week studying wilderness medicine. The class was held in the middle of winter. The two instructors were mountaineers with countless hours of experience saving lives and facing deaths in remote corners of the world. Simon was a Denali guy and Gabe did landmine work in Southeast Asia. Both climbed ice.

After lunch on the last day of the course Simon got quiet

and very serious. He said that now we had to talk about another aspect of the work and that if anybody didn't feel comfortable it was fine to leave the room. Nobody left. We all sat tight. Outside it was getting ready to storm, snow lightly falling, night only a few hours off. A fellow next to me, usually a fierce joker, put his hands on the table.

Simon said the other aspect of the work was trauma. He told a story about a plane crash. It was a commercial jet and a major American airport. It was many bodies. It was a heavy response, dozens and dozens of emergency personnel on site. He described how easily you get pulled into the situation, the flow of the disaster, everything that needs to be done and that you've been trained to do without thinking. And then it's finished, he said. You're at home on the couch. You're watching TV or having dinner or humming your kid a lullaby. You're chopping onions. You're at the edge of sleep.

Processing. That was the lesson. Having spent all week teaching us how to help people, how to assess their injuries, how to stabilize and evacuate, the last lesson was that sometimes you can't. I will repeat that: Sometimes you can't. Sometimes you arrive on the scene and the bodies are in pieces and the pieces are in pieces. Sometimes there's enough blood to drown in a thousand times, once nightly for years to come. You may have nightmares. The images may haunt you. Following that bad plane crash, Simon told us, the medical crews went through psychiatric evaluations and participated in discussion groups. They didn't just drift off. They knew that drifting off was not an option.

Remembering this lecture, I think of deer hunters. They *process* the meat. That's their word for bleeding and skinning and butchering and wrapping the cuts in plastic and paper and putting them in the garage chest freezer. For dating and naming the cuts with black ink. For turning a killing into another year's calories, into holiday feasts shared with family and friends. Processing. It's a method. It's been passed down the generations, season to season, hand to hand, father and mother to daughter and son.

Matt, a teacher I know, tells a story about a cow moose. He was leading a group of high school students on a camping trip in late spring. Exploring, they came upon a brook bridged by a fallen tree. The moose lay beneath the tree, partway in the water. What had happened? Maybe the tree fell on the moose while she was having a drink? The back end of the carcass was eaten clean, the skeleton chewed by coyotes and a long winter. The front end, protected by the log, was fur and flesh, a rotten mess feeding the soil. They lifted the log as a group and tugged the moose free, out of the brook and onto higher ground. They wanted to have a funeral.

"It was really beautiful," Matt recalls. "We went around the circle and everyone was given a chance to say something, whatever they wanted, or they could be silent when their turn came. One student said a prayer. I was blown away. I won't try to repeat it because I'll get it wrong. It was something like, *The moose is now able to complete its journey.* It was stirring and it was raw and it was beautiful. It was life and it was death. It was profound and it allowed students to participate in that larger dance."

Some of Matt's students have lost a parent. Some have lost siblings, aunts, uncles, friends. I picture their circle, the things said and not said, the quiet of springtime leaves speaking to other springtime leaves, the ghosts hovering close. Afternoon light slants to the glistening pelvis. The muzzle is huge and softening. The brook's voice fills each young ear.

"I think being able to witness the cycle of life and death as it appears in the natural world allows them to accept," Matt says. "Not to gloss over or forget or ignore, but to just accept."

~

Richard Nelson again: "The historical literature portrays Indians, above all, as masters of still hunting: a solitary man in the forest, armed with bow and arrow, slipping like a phantom through light and shadow, stopping every few yards to watch, waiting for the flicker of movement that reveals a deer, then cannily stalking within range. There is also a romantic but accurate image of the hunter disguised as his prey, covered with a whole or partial deer hide, his own head embellished with antlers." The Navajo, who practiced this style, would use "the sacred hide of a deer killed by suffocation rather than with arrows or bullets."

Suffocation? It sounds impossible. It's not. Deer are sprinters, but humans run longer, or at least we can. Open country, the red dirt and sagebrush, the monsoon thunderheads building from endless scrub. Hear the beat of your own feet, the uninterrupted drumming. You follow the buck. You follow and follow. You gain inches until you are within inches, and now you can almost touch the running back, the ears, the breathing chest. Crushing the sagebrush, freeing the scent together, the two of you move in sync, human matching deer and deer matching human, mile after mile.

Nelson quotes writer Barre Toelken: "When the deer is finally caught he is thrown to the ground as gently as possible, his mouth and nose are held shut, and covered with a handful of pollen so that he may die breathing the sacred substance."

A snort, a golden cloud-puff of pollen. Dust hangs in a lens over the shuddering embrace.

"And then—I am not sure how widespread this is with the Navajos—one sings to the deer as it is dying, and apologizes ritually for taking its life, explaining that he needs the skin for his family."

~

Four or five days before Simon's lecture on trauma, during an anatomy lesson, he mentioned a time teaching a class when he'd come across a dead deer in the woods. He brought the students out and they put on gloves and inspected the body. It was a great success, the dead animal bringing to life what can be so much jargon, so much diagramming on the page or blackboard. The smell of late autumn, the foliage and distant smoke and hardness to the air. I see them circled up, crouched down, quiet and attentive. I see Simon bending forward. The windpipe worked, he said. You could push air into the lungs and they would fill.

~

I have tried to say goodbye. I have tried, many ways, many times, to say goodbye.

Once, on my way to the lake for a swim, I hit a chipmunk. It was a summer day, hot and humid. Besides a speck of blood at the mouth, the chipmunk seemed intact, normal. I searched the car for something to use as a bag, but all I could find was an old foam sandal. I slid the chipmunk onto the sandal and took the body with me to the beach. Sitting shirtless on blue stones, using a jackknife and some twigs, I dissected the chipmunk. I looked inside the chipmunk. I will repeat that: I looked inside.

A few weeks later, my dog killed a chipmunk and brought the body to me. She had been chasing the chipmunk around a shagbark hickory and then the chipmunk was in her mouth and then the chipmunk was at my feet. I sharpened a knife from the kitchen and collected some other instruments, some pins, tweezers, two of those spikes with yellow plastic handles used for eating corn on the cob. I went to the beach. I was supposed to meet friends for a dip. When they arrived I had the pelt laid across a log, the guts in a neat pile for the birds.

The rest of that summer I drove with a dissection kit in my car. I got a real scalpel and some latex gloves. I was always nervous about making the initial incision. I remember cutting into an eyeball and recoiling as a stream of fluid burst out. I remember realizing that every creature is made of layers.

Another summer, working for the Forest Service in Arizona, I collected skulls and smaller bones. The pile in the weeds outside my cabin door grew with each passing hike. Scapula. Vertebrae. Ribs. I found dead sparrows on the dirt road and caged them in chicken wire so that they could decompose without the local scavengers stealing them. I picked a squirrel up and put him in a cinder block's hollow and checked his progress daily. When the field season ended I strung all my bones on bits of clear fishing line, then climbed a ponderosa pine and decorated the tree. It was a mobile. Maybe a hundred floating pieces.

That same summer my girlfriend hit a jackrabbit. It was her first roadkill. The moon was in the rearview mirror, the sky purple, the windows down. The rabbit jumped out and was tossed up and we heard a sound. I wrote my girlfriend a poem. The sound was in the poem. She cried.

I have sat for hours, the scatter of teeth and stink of flesh all around. I have sat this way with no intention, with no thoughts in my mind, with an inability to rise.

~

They tell us that life lives off life, feeds off life, trails death everywhere it goes. That's just how it is, they insist. You can wear a mask to avoid inhaling insects. You can sweep the ground before your crushing foot lands. You can go vegetarian, go vegan, and still you will fail. But you should not call it failure. You should call it life, living, dying, the world being the world. The most we can do is pause, pray, give thanks, apologize, make ceremonies, make them a part of the very life that kills other lives.

The deer die and the blood is on our hands, the shards of bone splintering memory. This is far from new. We've been killing deer for millennia. We will not claw our way out of the cycle. Only by clawing our way deeper into the cycle might we find some peace, a place to rest. Perhaps our efforts won't ever feel like enough. Perhaps there is no place to rest. Perhaps it is hard, hard, hard indeed.

I accept.

But there is something else going on here. The word is "accident," car *accident*. The slaughter is unintentional, and when the slaughter is unintentional the slaughter becomes even worse because we have no ability to process the slaughter, no ritual by which to share and address the pain. A nice dinner. A couple beers. A basketball game and some shut-eye. Then nightmares, twisted sleep, sorrow in the chest. Tears falling to raised hands.

And there is this, too: What if the doe is not a deer? What if the doe is an aquifer, an ocean, the night's own private darkness? What if the doe is the black soil? What if the doe is the chirps and growls and heavy breath, the canyons and forests and ridgelines, the ice, the plankton, the drifting seed? What if the car that hits the doe is a light switch, a faucet, a new shirt? A government? An economy? What if the car is our everyday experience, our reality, our modern way, and what if it is constantly murdering the smooth brown bodies we love?

What if there is no backing out, no making things right? What happens if we ignore all of this? What happens then?

~

Jennifer let go of her hands and the blanket caught them. Morning in New Jersey. Windows not yet bright with sun. I sat down and Lucy, the dog, ran in from the hall and leapt onto the couch, snuggling between us.

"In the middle of the night I woke up crying," Jennifer said. "I was sobbing and I couldn't stop. Do you think that deer is going to die?"

There was nothing to say, but I said something anyway. Something. Anything. And as I was speaking Jennifer's tears dried on her cheeks and Mike came out from the bedroom and Lucy rolled onto her back, making us laugh. And we all spoke, though I forget what we said. And then I got up to start the coffee. And I made a lot and I made it strong. And in my head, as I waited for the pot to fill, leaning against the kitchen counter, my bare feet on the cold tile floor, I sang that gentle tune, the tune for the doe, the song of goodbye, which I still remember today.

~     ~     ~

# *Where I Write*

I would like to say that my feet know the narrow dirt path better than they know my socks. I would like to say that the path curves into a birch grove floored with ferns and after precisely 103 paces reaches a hut above a stream. I would like to say that inside this hut I sit on a hard chair at a clean desk and write essays, articles, stories, and poems. That I have a place, that I go there daily to relish its moods and variations, that I work there, that the place works through me and back out onto the page—these are things I would like to say. But I will not say them. Because I am not a liar.

I am, as a friend recently put it, a wandering fool.

The first prose I ever published was written on a home-made raft that measured five feet by seven feet. I was living on the raft, drifting and rowing and sailing the length of Vermont's summery Lake Champlain. This special raft of mine was thin, sensitive, and the slightest wave wobbled my script. I took breaks from scribbling, sharpened my pencil. Dunked my head, came up dripping. Ten days into the voyage, tracing a random stretch of shoreline with the finished piece, I hailed a farmer soaking his toes who said he would be happy to deliver it to the Burlington newspaper. Onward from there.

In San Francisco, I found myself repeatedly walking forty rainy blocks to the public library, backpack stuffed with peanut butter sandwiches and a laptop. I always ate the sandwiches in the too-warm hallway near the basement bathroom, then climbed the stairs to my favorite table. Sometimes my feet touched the feet of strangers beneath the table: old men with funny ears, young ladies studying medical texts, children squirming from boredom or delight, schizophrenics mumbling into their fat novels. Wearing headphones, I listened to the same four minutes of looping Russian choral music, week after week. I didn't get a lot of writing done, distracted more often than not by books about sea lions, mountaineers, bristlecone pines, hermits, and environmental catastrophes.

My favorite office to date smelled of detergent—a laundry room in the wilderness. For four springs and four summers I resided at a Forest Service field station on the Kaibab Plateau, just north of the Grand Canyon. This remote laundry room was furnished with a washing machine and dryer, of course, but also a hard chair, a clean desk. The acoustics were interesting—bouncy, bright—and I liked to hum my sentences and paragraphs into existence. Out the window, in the siding of a neighboring cabin, a family of wrens came and went from their knothole nest. Birdsong overlaid my song, as well as the churning song of the washer and the droning song of the dryer. There were lovely harmonies to explore in that room. And sunrise-pink light. And hours of effort.

As for that perfect studio-shack, that snug hut in the woods—I'm hoping to buy land, clear brush, make it happen. Carpenters speak of building "from the ground up," and that seems an appropriate practice for a writer interested in nature. Until then, I'll take whatever I can get, whatever's offered. A tent in Scotland. A dormitory in Antarctica. The Embassy Suites. The leeward side of a summit boulder. Lakeview, Montana. Lamy, New Mexico. Ponds and marshes. Curbs and benches. Low autumn light hitting my good friend's deck at a slant, hitting his sleepy border collie, hitting the clinking ice cubes in my glass.

Last month: my mother's garage. Next month: a slick-rock alcove, a foam Therm-a-Rest pad, a hooded jacket. Tonight, on the New Jersey shore, Atlantic City's skyline glows neon beyond the bay of crying gulls.

What are they crying about? How did I get here? Who's winning at the casino? When will I leave?

Oh, these are question only a liar could answer. The gulls, the ocean, the notebook on the blue bedspread, the spider on the blue wall. It's not my home, not my place, but it'll do. For now. For a wandering fool.

# Credits and Acknowledgments

First, I'd like to thank those involved with the publications where many of the pieces first appeared: Steve Casimiro, Sean Prentiss, Tyler Cohen, Victoria Schlesinger, Moises Velasquez-Manoff, Dan Rademacher, Donald McNutt, Peter Gurche, Danny Kuzio, Jodi Peterson, Michelle Nijhuis, Diane Sylvain, Brian Calvert, Bruce Jennings, Scott Gast, Diana Owen, Hannah Fries, Tara Rae Miner, Jonah Ogles, Chris Keyes, Elizabeth Hightower, Will Gordon, Carol Ann Fitzgerald, Sy Safransky, and Lisa Lynn. There are countless others working behind the scenes at these publications, helping connect writers with readers, and I'm sorry not to know each and every name.

Second, I'd like to thank the new friends, old friends, experts, colleagues, and random strangers who have served as resources for my writing projects. Included in this category are the authors I've quoted or referenced in my work. In particular, though, I'm thinking of the people who have generously allowed me to ask questions and take notes. Your openness to being followed around and turned into characters on the page is integral.

Third, I'd like to thank the team at Trinity University Press: Steffanie Mortis, Tom Payton, Sarah Nawrocki,

Burgin Streetman, Christi Stanforth. I appreciate your support of writers interested in, for lack of a better phrase, environmental nonfiction. Keep going. More books, please.

Fourth, I'd like to thank my kind family, my funny and adventurous buddies, my various literary and scientific mentors, and everybody else who has encouraged my pursuit of a life devoted to engaging, via experience and thought, the world of nature, the nature of the world. You know who you are.

Finally, I'd like to thank the land's creatures, by which I mean not only squirrels and marmots and minnows and ants and woodpeckers and warblers, but also trees and boulders, melting snowfields and jumpy creeks, strange weathers and stunning sunsets. Honestly, it annoys me when authors publicly extend their gratitude beyond the human realm, yet there's absolutely no denying that without places, especially places in the American West—without this earth—I'd be in a different business. People make books, true, but something else makes people. Thanks to *something else.*

~

The essays in this book were previously published in the following publications and are reprinted here with thanks (and, in some cases, revisions, including altered titles).

*Adventure Journal,* "In Praise of Scrambling"

*Backcountry Magazine,* "Pooh Bear in Yellowstone"

*Bay Nature,* "A Room of Boughs in a City of Lights," "Birdnap"

*Blueline,* "Addressing the Forces That Would Destroy Us and Everything We Love"

*Camas,* "Thoughts after an Owl"

*Coachella Review,* "Big Canyon"

*Cross Country Skier,* "Grandma's Deep Winter Kaibab Adventure"

*High Country News,* "Stucco'd All Over," "Watching Goggles," "The Anthropological Aesthetic," "Listening to Big Empty," "The Irrigator's Club," "Relittering," "When We Curse Peaks," "Wild Reading," "Doug"

*Minding Nature,* "Letter to the Megalopolis"

*Orion Magazine,* "The Drop," "Secret Springs," "Somewhere in the Middle of Nowhere," "Flying with Birds," "Creeking," "Adjusting Monty," "Where I Write," "Nature-Loving Beards," "Things I Won't Say about Wilderness"

*Outside,* "Favor the Mountain," "The Unknown Country"

*The Sun,* "Ways to Take Your Coffee," "Write-Ins for President"

*Vermont Sports,* "Old Friend"

LEATH TONINO, a writer from Vermont, has also worked as a wildlife biologist in Arizona, a blueberry farmer in New Jersey, and a snow shoveler in Antarctica. He is the author of *The Animal One Thousand Miles Long: Seven Lengths of Vermont and Other Adventures,* and his work has appeared in magazines such as *Outside, Men's Journal, Orion, Tricycle, Utne Reader,* and *The Sun.* When not at his desk, he roams North America's libraries and wildlands.